The Complete Guide to Chakras

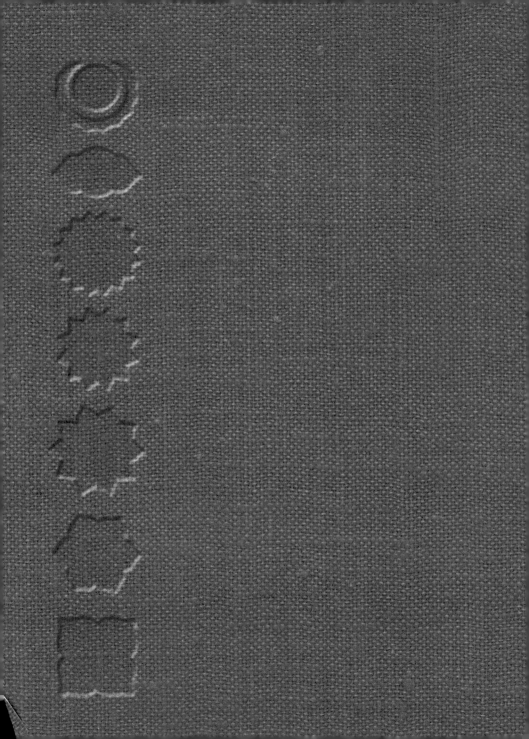

The COMPLETE GUIDE to CHaKras

Unleash the positive power within

Ambika Wauters

NEW BURLINGTON

A QUARTO BOOK

Published in 2018 by
New Burlington Press
The Old Brewery
6 Blundell Street
London N7 9BH

ISBN-13: 978-1-84566-407-7
ISBN-10: 1-84566-407-8

Conceived, designed,
and produced by
Quarto Publishing plc
The Old Brewery
6 Blundell Street
London N7 9BH

QUA: CGHC

Editor & designer: Michelle Pickering
Art director: Caroline Guest

Creative director: Moira Clinch
Publisher: Paul Carslake

Color separation by Modern Age
Repro House Ltd., Hong Kong
Printed by Toppan Leefung
Printers Ltd., China

CONTENTS

This book offers the possibility of opening a new dimension of healing and growth for you. It delves into the nature of the human energy system and illustrates how our energy can be expanded and transformed through healing the seven major energy centers, also known as chakras.

INTRODUCTION

Ganesha, the Hindu elephant god, is associated with wisdom. He is the protector and guardian of the Root Chakra.

WHAT ARE CHAKRAS?

The chakras are the key to physical health, emotional stability, and mental clarity. They act as conductors, filtering energy from the heavens and earth so that they can combine. The convergence of these energy fields forms a chakra. It is a vortex of moving energy, which then stimulates various endocrine organs in the body to secrete hormones into the blood system. (These are known as ductless glands, because their secretions go directly into the bloodstream.) The effects of hormones control our body. They also affect our state of mind.

Try to imagine the chakras as a "filtration system." It purifies our energy from the gross, physical plane associated with our primal instincts and basic animal nature, turning it into the highly refined, spiritual plane that connects us with the source of life itself. When we begin the journey through the chakras, we open the way for healing, psychological development, and spiritual growth to happen.

CHAKRA HEALING

As we progress upward through the energy centers, we learn more about who we are, and can transform and heal our energy levels. This enables us to become more focused on the paths we choose in order to fulfill ourselves; we realize our talents and gifts and allow love and compassion to become the center of our lives.

This system of healing is ancient. In many early cultures, energy was appreciated and refined until a person obtained mastery on the physical plane and could ascend to higher planes of consciousness. Today, in our highly charged world, we are in need of understanding this ancient knowledge about energy so that we can take charge of our lives and change the way we do things.

RADIANT ENERGY

As you read this book you will be invited to work with the affirmations, meditations, and exercises that have been created for all of the chakras. As you discover more about who you are, give yourself time to assimilate your insights. As you acknowledge your desire to make your life more fulfilled, you may get a deep sense of your own purpose for being here on the planet at this time.

This book is designed to bring healing and joy into your life. It can help you expand your way of looking at your life and empower you to transform the negative and less wholesome aspects of yourself until your energy shines and you are the radiant light you are meant to be.

There are seven chakras that are located up the body from the Root Chakra at the base of the spine to the Crown Chakra at the crown of the head.

Crown
Chakra

Brow
Chakra

Throat
Chakra

Heart
Chakra

Solar
Plexus
Chakra

Sacral
Chakra

Root
Chakra

the Chakra System

The chakra system is a model for the flow of subtle energy that runs through all life and through the human energy system. It is like a ladder that takes us from the physical realm of substance up through the workings of the higher mind and spirit, and into the realm of divine consciousness.

The phrase "subtle energy" refers to the force field surrounding all living things. In the human body, it comprises the aura and seven layers of energy that are referred to as the "subtle bodies." These control our physical well-being, emotional stability, and mental clarity. They are a direct reflection of our spiritual state and mirror how we feel about ourselves and life in general.

Subtle Energy

LIFE FORCE

Even though subtle energy is not visible, it can be experienced. It is apparent in people and can be felt by the light, open quality they have or by their negative demeanor. Even though we cannot see their energy, we perceive the quality of their energy field through their body language, the brightness or dullness in their eyes, the clarity or confusion of their minds, and by the things they say and do. Subtle energy pervades every interaction we have; it is the life force exchanged between us.

THE AURA

The aura is the energetic envelope that sheathes the body of any living thing. It acts as a bubble to enclose the energy field and protect the life force. It is the encasement that enables energy to circulate through living systems.

The layers of atmosphere form an aura of energy that keeps oxygen in circulation. Its purpose is to ensure life, so that we can breathe, and it keeps out harmful rays from the sun. When the aura is weakened by disease or distress, it is unable to hold its full capacity of energy. An example is the hole in the ozone layer that allows harmful ultraviolet radiation into the atmosphere.

A compromised aura in the human energy system does something similar when it is distressed. Having a strong and viable energy field ensures against external invasion, which can take the form of psychic attack and even physical disease. If our aura is weak, we can strengthen it with positive thinking, meditation, and prayer. Living a healthy lifestyle also builds a strong aura.

POSITIVE INTENTION

In humans, the aura is made up of several layers of subtle energy. There are seven energy bodies in total that affect every state of our being. Each layer acts as a filter for life energy. They exist at a gross, physical level and proceed to more differentiated and refined layers of energy.

Energy moves up from the earth into our lower chakras and affects our physical bodies. It also moves down from the cosmos through our upper chakras and affects our thinking, feelings, and spiritual perception. We can transform our energy through awareness and by understanding how the life force responds to positive intention.

Experiencing Subtle Energy

This is one way in which you can experience subtle energy. Begin by rubbing your hands briskly together and holding them a few inches from one another. Feel the heat that emanates from them. That heat is subtle energy. It can be used for healing pain, emotional dysfunction, and mental imbalance. It is imprinted with your spirit and the thoughts and feelings you have. The more positive your thoughts, the stronger your energy field.

Subtle energy is all around us. It pervades all nature, and infuses the etheric realms of life with vitality and life force.

The colors of the rainbow are the same as the colors in the chakras of the human energy system. Red has the densest energy and corresponds to the magnet earth energies, while violet, which is the least dense, relates to the electric, cosmic end of the spectrum.

THE SEVEN LAYERS OF THE AURA

The layers of the aura correspond to the seven planes through which we have our being. From the top down they are the Divine, the Monadic, the Spiritual, the Mental, the Emotional, the Etheric, and the Physical. All these bodies are enveloped within the auric sheath. This sheath is called the condula. Each plane is divided into seven sub-planes, giving us 49 planes of energetic activity in all.

DIVINE AND MONADIC

The highest plane is the Divine plane, where the Godhead is experienced. Below it is the Monadic plane, which is the vehicle the soul uses to express itself. It is said that the soul uses the lower planes to develop experience and maturity for its growth and healing.

SPIRITUAL, MENTAL, AND EMOTIONAL

The Spiritual body functions as a conduit to our higher aspects through meditation, prayer, and inner reflection. The Mental body is made up of our attitudes about life. The Emotional body opens up as we become more sensitive and trust our feelings to act as inner guidance. It corresponds to our awareness of self as valuable and good, worthy of love, kindness, and respect. It is made up of our desires and, as a result of our incessant longings, is very volatile. It is in this plane that disease originates that can deeply affect our physical health. It is through the Emotional body that we experience the range of opposites, such as pleasure and pain, fear and courage, attachment and disengagement. This is where energy gets blocked and imploded when our all-consuming desires run our lives.

ETHERIC AND PHYSICAL

The Etheric body is the thickest and densest of the subtle bodies. It vitalizes and energizes the Physical body and connects us with the cycles and rhythms of earth energy. The chakras exist in the Etheric body, next to the Physical body. The chakras stimulate the ductless glands (endocrine organs that are known as ductless glands because they secrete directly into the bloodstream) of the Physical body, which produce different states of health, depending on our feelings and attitudes. The Physical body contains all our organic systems and is composed of gases, liquids, and dense matter. It is on this plane that the spirit can express itself, learn the lessons of life, and cultivate wisdom.

All the bodies interact within themselves. They are highly differentiated fields of energy where our spirit, our feelings, and our body act as one. Body/mind/spirit is one continuum without separation.

The atmosphere surrounding the earth holds in vital gases that sustain life on our planet. The aura acts in a similar way by enveloping our vital life energy so that we can grow, thrive, and develop to our fullest potential.

VISUALIZING THE AURA

Step 1

Imagine a photograph of the earth with layers of atmosphere surrounding the globe. These layers hold the essential gases needed for life. Without an energetic envelope surrounding the planet, there would be no atmosphere. Our planet would be without life.

Step 2

Visualize the same sort of envelope around your body. It extends about 8 in. (20 cm) from the surface of your body. It contains all the vital energy you need to live. You can expand this field by thinking positive and loving thoughts, such as "I am love" and "I love myself," repeatedly. You can also shrink this field by thinking negative thoughts. Each time you affirm your being, you contribute to your overall health and well-being.

Step 3

You can attempt to visualize the entire planet embraced within your auric field. This way you are one with all life. Doing this visualization daily will expand your aura. If you practice in front of a mirror, you may be able to see your energy field form around you. This atmospheric layer expands and contracts in response to your thoughts.

Wheels of Light

The word chakra comes from the ancient Sanskrit and means "wheel of light." It refers to the spinning vortex of energy created when magnet energy from the molten core of the earth rises up and meets electric energy descending from the cosmos. This wheel, made up of both these forces, propels our life force. It is said that minerals and crystals contain one chakra that conducts energy in and out of their substance; animals have up to three; and humans have seven major and twenty-one minor chakras, and all the acupuncture points also act as chakras. As we continue to evolve and become more sensitive to energy, we will cultivate new chakras to process refined energy layers.

THE HUMAN ENERGY SYSTEM

The human energy system comprises seven layers of energy bodies within the aura. The chakras exist in the first layer of subtle energy and act as conductors for energy to move through all layers of the aura. Their health and integrity are maintained through a grounded lifestyle and positive and loving thoughts toward the self and the world.

CHAKRA QUALITIES

This manner of comprehending energy is based on the ancient knowledge that all life is energetic and spiritual in origin. The ancients modeled the chakra system on a complete acceptance that man and earth were one and inseparable. Each chakra, or energy center, is linked to an element. The earth element, for instance, is associated with the Root Chakra. This chakra sits at the base of the spine and conducts energy into the hips, legs, and feet. It connects us to the earth and its field. Through the Root Chakra, we are anchored physically in our bodies and supplied with the life force we need to maintain and support our lives.

Each chakra corresponds with many different qualities and substances. For instance, each chakra resonates with a color and a musical note. We find affinities to specific crystals, gemstones, and even plants. The ancients made up myths to connect the chakras with archetypal characteristics so that people could understand the life issues and qualities that were associated with each vital life center.

ENERGY LEVELS

The chakras comprise various levels of awareness, activity, and energetic charge. For instance, the Root Chakra is red and has a very dense vibration. It affects our ability to be present in our body and produces the vitality that we need to stay alive. Toward the other end of the energy spectrum, the Brow Chakra vibrates to affect our mental and spiritual processes. It resonates with a different musical note and has an affinity to the color blue.

MASCULINE AND FEMININE

The lower chakras fall into the category of magnetic energy, whereas the upper chakras are electrical in nature. The lower three chakras, which sit below the diaphragm, are known as the feminine chakras because their function is specifically receptive. They take in energy from the earth and the immediate environment. They link us with Mother Earth and the events and qualities that tie us to family, clan, tribe, and community. They concern themselves with how we master life through our instincts, using inherited ancestral energy to maintain our life force. These chakras also carry the patterns for disease and health, as well as the courage, cunning, and stealth required to stay alive.

The upper four chakras are known as the masculine chakras. They are primarily concerned with giving energy out in the form of love, communication, healthy attitudes, and inner reflection. They link us with the source and become active as we become spiritual and capable of love.

These chakras are all interdependent. When one energy center is shut down, others will compensate in maintaining the life force. They have defined boundaries that distinguish one from another. The various parts of the energy system are interlinked to maintain the continuum of life.

The chakras are an ancient model that describe the human energy system in its various components. This model originated in India perhaps as long as 25,000 years ago.

Chakras are nonanatomical in nature. They exist in the energy body known as the Etheric body that, as we have seen on page 13, is the layer of energy closest to the Physical body.

CHAKRA FUNCTIONS

All energy moves in spirals. This wheel describes the action of energy in the chakras. Water is the element that governs the function of the Sacral Chakra, and has a strong affinity with our emotions.

ENERGY CONDUCTORS

The chakras penetrate all seven layers of the aura. They act as conductors, drawing vital energy up from the earth, circulating it through the Physical body, and releasing it as higher awareness. In other words, vitality is transmuted into awareness, spirituality, and a deeper conception of the universe. Likewise, cosmic energy moves down through the Crown Chakra and manifests as right action, creativity, and health.

As we develop our consciousness and refine our sensitivities, we release old, stagnant emotional energy in the form of dreams, memories, and feelings that weigh down our spirit. The more freedom, love, and beauty the spirit experiences, the wider the energy fields become. As we evolve, we actually become healthier.

LIVING IN THE PRESENT

The process of opening up to greater energy fields occurs as we live fully in the present. The state of our chakras is very important. They are the vital key to what we think and feel. They are the ladder of love that takes us from the lowest and most base aspect of life that is concerned with survival, to the highest realm of consciousness, healing, and bliss.

Our chakras are the repositories of our thoughts, feelings, and attitudes about life. If we have narrow ideas about life and limit our existence, then our energy field will be small and narrow. Without the adequate amounts of vital energy, we fall into physical and psychological imbalance.

ACTIVITY LEVELS

The chakras form a well-organized system that keeps the life force directed, economical, and fluid. When something happens to impede the flow of life energy, the chakras slow down activity, and energy becomes sluggish and even stagnant. If this situation is temporary, the energy resumes its natural flow. If the situation continues for some time, the chakras need stimulation to become active again. Our health and well-being depend on active chakras.

CHAKRA ACTIVITIES

Root Chakra: Draws energy from the earth's magnetic core; stimulates aggressive drives linked to survival; anchors our spirit in our worldly existence.

Sacral Chakra: Promotes our ability to enjoy life in physical ways; governs our well-being, our sense of deserving a good life, and our capacity to develop a sense of abundance.

Solar Plexus Chakra: Relates to self-value, confidence, self esteem, and freedom of choice; reflects how we see ourselves and exercise our innate power.

Heart Chakra: Keeps the life force alive; moves love through our lives; shields heart from emotional pain; thought to be the seat of divinity within us.

Throat Chakra: Directs the life force toward creativity, self-expression, truth, and integrity; controls our ability to communicate clearly.

Brow Chakra: Center of our innate intelligence; thrives on the distilled wisdom of our losses and pain; seeks meaning, truth, and freedom.

Crown Chakra: Center of bliss, beauty, and spirituality; allows us to deepen our connection with the source of our being; influences inner cycles, such as sleep and happiness.

Archetypes and Chakras

Archetypes have emerged out of the core of human experience to represent the good and bad qualities in us all. Each archetype symbolizes a quintessential pattern of energy that describes a set of fixed patterns of behavior. In the case of the chakras, each archetype refers to a level of personal responsibility, a degree of empowerment, and a quantity of energy and vitality. Each chakra has a positive archetype and a negative one, corresponding to the qualities and challenges associated with that chakra. These archetypes are transformed by conscious awareness. The more responsibility we take for our personal archetypes, the more empowered we are and the more energy we have available for our health, creativity, and joy. Recognizing our negativity opens the chakra and psychologically empowers us and revitalizes our health. When we begin to take responsibility for the negative attitudes that block our aliveness and happiness, we heal an aspect of ourselves and move onto higher ground.

Positive Archetypes

Root Chakra: The Mother
Nurturing, self-sufficient, responsible

Sacral Chakra: The Emperor/Empress
Pleasure, abundance, enjoyment

Solar Plexus Chakra: The Warrior
Confident, creative, courageous

Heart Chakra: The Lover
Generosity, openness, loving, good will

Throat Chakra: The Communicator
Outspoken, truthful, open

Brow Chakra: The Wise Person
Flexibility, humor, cultivation of wisdom

Crown Chakra: The Guru
Cultivation of grace, bliss, gratitude; acknowledging divine intervention

Negative Archetypes

Root Chakra: The Victim
Lacking energy, empowerment, and life force

Sacral Chakra: The Martyr
Critical, sour, condemning

Solar Plexus Chakra: The Servant
Needy, seeking approval, unempowered

Heart Chakra: The Actor/Actress
Conditional love, bound by convention

Throat Chakra: The Silent Child
Suppressed communication, unexpressed emotions

Brow Chakra: The Intellectual
Rational, factual, rigid, dry

Crown Chakra: The Egotist
Arrogance, self-absorption, inflexibility

CHAKRAS AND THE PHYSICAL BODY

The vital force of the human energy system directs energy through the layers of subtle energy bodies. It is the living part of us that moves our limbs, and lets us feel emotions and make free choices. It animates our minds and preserves us under stress. The vital force exists in all life forms and is the same whether found in a human being, an animal, or a plant. It is different in form, but is the same force in all living things.

This force directs our physical energies, using the chakras as conductors to filter energy through the physical body. Energy moves through the chakras, stimulating hormone flow in the ductless glands. These, in turn, affect the biochemistry of the body and the rate at which the body uses energy. At a physical level, this is called metabolism.

ENERGETIC MAPS

When our body stores excess heat or fluid, it affects the way the body processes energy. Too much heat, which may be unexpressed anger, causes inflammation of the blood. Too much fluid stagnation in the body causes catarrh and excess mucus and can turn into tumors if not reversed.

Our physical bodies are energetic maps. The body has no mind of its own, but acts as a mirror for the higher mind, showing us where there is imbalance. We need to read the body as a map of emotional suppression to understand what is going on at a deep level. It shows where there is constriction, or not enough energy in the system.

The vital force exists in all life forms, whether human being, animal, or plant. It distinguishes life from nonlife.

PHYSICAL ENERGIES OF THE CHAKRAS

Root Chakra: Adrenals
The fight-or-flight function of the kidneys is activated.

Sacral Chakra: Ovaries/testes
The reproductive organs that control sexual development.

Solar Plexus Chakra: Pancreas
The organ that processes sugar. It also controls the digestion of food.

Heart Chakra: Thymus
Building a strong immunity from pain and disease.

Throat Chakra: Thyroid
Controls metabolism and affects physical and mental development.

Brow Chakra: Pituitary
Influences metabolism, growth, and other hormones, including those connected with giving birth.

Crown Chakra: Pineal
Produces melatonin and regulates our body clock.

The Sphinx represents the spiritual enigma of humanity. It has the body of a beast and the head of a human. As we ascend the human energy system, we follow the process of evolution from our animal nature to our spiritual capacity for love, joy, and healing.

THE HEALING POWER OF ENERGY

The body uses energy released from the chakras. If the chakra is congested, energy filtration becomes sluggish. This may be experienced as coldness and lack of vital energy. We may feel tired, out of sorts, or constipated. Too much energy in the chakra appears as heat, irritability, and stagnation.

You are advised to consult your physician if you are experiencing any discomfort in these chakra areas. You may also wish to seek out healthy alternatives for relief from your condition. Please refer to the chapter on healing (see pages 126–141). Sometimes conditions respond to new ways of thinking. If you have had a condition for many years, it may be useful to examine your life to see what you were experiencing emotionally at the onset of your physical problems.

The innate healing power of the body is stimulated by energetic treatments. Once you have identified the physical complaints you have with the governing chakra, you can use the affirmations and meditations in this book to bring balance and harmony back in alignment with your higher purpose.

CHAKRAS AND THE EMOTIONAL BODY

The emotions have a profound effect on our healing. They come from our desires and attachments to how we expect our life to be fulfilled. If we are unhappy about a situation, we experience aggression, anxiety, or grief. Whether we are conscious of those feelings and are able to allow them a space in our experience is going to affect energy levels. Suppressing feelings locks them into the subconscious, where they congest the energy flow from the chakras.

Reanimating a deadened feeling function can create anxiety because we are not used to the sensation that feelings create. We need to find appropriate ways of allowing our feelings room in our life. If we swallow our grief and hide our fear, we deny ourselves an opportunity for growth. If we pretend that everything is fine in our life, we cut ourselves off from our own aliveness.

MANAGING EMOTIONS

Learning how to manage our emotions comes with practice and maturity. When we know what we are feeling, we can choose appropriate avenues of expression. In the end, emotions are simply energy. How we express that energy is our choice. The chakras are extremely responsive to what we think and feel. Unexpressed anger or frustration can accumulate as tension in the muscles. Imploded emotional energy can also overcharge the chakra system, causing imbalance and preventing us from using our energy in a positive way.

When we harness our vital energy to our willpower, we develop the capacity to move with grace, precision, and intent.

EMOTIONAL ENERGIES OF THE CHAKRAS

Root Chakra: Aggression, anger, violence, jealousy.

Sacral Chakra: Pleasure, feeling good, deservedness, joy/feeling bad, envious, not caring for your physical body.

Solar Plexus Chakra: Self-worth, confidence, power, clear choices for selfhood.

Heart Chakra: Being capable of love and compassion for self and others.

Throat Chakra: Releasing feelings through expressing yourself, including crying, shouting, laughing, and saying that you are not happy.

Brow Chakra: Giving yourself permission to experience your feelings. Choosing when it is appropriate to express them.

Crown Chakra: Wanting to cultivate bliss and surrender to what is.

MENTAL ENERGIES OF THE CHAKRAS

Root Chakra: Attitudes of separation, exclusivity, territory, belonging, your right to your own space.

Sacral Chakra: Attitudes of being and having enough, knowing that you deserve the life you say you want, enjoyment and well-being, delighting in good health.

Solar Plexus Chakra: Attitudes of being well with yourself and knowing your worth, linking into your personal power, which comes from an affirmed sense of selfhood.

Heart Chakra: Attitudes of happiness, joy, and delight, knowing what makes your heart sing, embracing life.

Throat Chakra: Having a sense that expressing your truth is your key to individuality. Speaking the truth, not gossiping, lying, exaggerating.

Brow Chakra: Attitudes that are self-confirming, accepting, inclusive. Developing understanding for your own limitations and those of others, cultivating gratitude.

Crown Chakra: Developing holistic and universal principles of acceptance, respect, and knowing that we never do anything without the help of a higher source.

CHAKRAS AND THE MENTAL BODY

The ideas and attitudes we have reflect how we were raised: what our families thought about life, what our churches and schools felt was right, and what our culture honored as valuable. We accumulate many self-limiting ideas based on what others perceive to be right. Learning to think for ourselves takes time, many mistakes, and a commitment to life. When we develop wholesome beliefs that reflect a peaceful inner state, our thinking becomes clearer and we become less opinionated about how things should be. The more positive they are, the more resilient our energy system.

Learning new skills is a function of a healthy Brow Chakra. It gives the mind energy to clear a visible path for our life to follow, so our gifts and talents can be cultivated.

Visualizing a Chakra

- *A chakra is divided into three sections: the outer lip, the body, and the tip, containing the seeds of our destiny. The outer lip of the chakra acts as a filter to our daily exchanges with our surroundings. If our feelings remain unexpressed, this energy accumulates and congests our energy system. This is what is called energetic dross, and it builds up, causing symptoms of fatigue, aging, and illness.*

- *The main body of the chakra is made up of a fine web of etheric energy. It is composed of the warp and weave of our thoughts and attitudes. If we feel a particular way about something, it will affect how we respond emotionally and, therefore, energetically.*

- *At the very core (or tip) of the chakra is the seed of our destiny. This seed cannot be opened until our negativity and self-limiting ideas have been removed, because they block our energy. Once we begin the inner work of affirming our being and honoring who we are, our destiny begins to unfold. Life changes for us in palpable ways. There are more of the good things we enjoy: more love, more abundance, more awareness.*

- *As we affirm our worth and our choices for health, abundance, and ease, life responds to what we think about ourselves. People who do affirm themselves find that life does become easier and there is enough. Energy follows thought, and, as we open ourselves to what is good and positive, destiny unfolds as it was meant to. Health, joy, prosperity, and well-being emerge out of knowing that we deserve the life we say we want.*

- *We direct our destiny by managing the ways we think. We either become inner-directed, knowing our worth and goodness and experiencing ourselves as enough, or we become outer-directed and dictated to by family pressure and social and religious standards.*

Core or tip

Body   Outer lip

A chakra resembles a large cone. The outer lip catches the accumulated stress of the day. The long body is made of the attitudes and ideas we have about life. The seeds of our destiny lie in the very tip of the chakra and cannot be opened until we have harvested out our negativity about life.

The realm of the spirit opens us to the all-pervading consciousness of truth, love, and wisdom. It gives our lives purpose and teaches us to honor our own inner guidance for living. The chakras respond in a sensitive and intelligent manner to our thoughts and attitudes. They reflect the nature of our belief system by the levels of energy they filter. We have either an expanded or limited energy field in accordance with those attitudes.

the SPIRITUAL DIMENSION

THE POWER OF THOUGHT
Most of us do not reflect on our basic beliefs, and yet, if we were to look at how we judge ourselves and limit our sense of joy and well-being, we might understand how we also limit our energy. Self-examination can help increase our vitality, health, and happiness. When attitudes become unbending, the energetic counterpart occurs in the chakras and manifests in our body. If our attitudes are too rigid or too unstructured, our chakras will be exactly the same. Energy follows thought as a river follows its course.

If, for instance, we harbor a belief that life is difficult and we should avoid risks, our energy system will show constraint, limitation, and diminished energy flow, particularly in the first three chakras that hold the unconscious attitudes of family, clan, and community. If we believe that life can prevail and we are willing to take a risk, we will be blessed with the energy we need.

CHAKRA INTELLIGENCE

Each chakra has a form of intelligence that allows it to organize energy according to its higher purpose. When we cultivate grounded ideas and wholesome attitudes about ourselves, the chakras perform optimally. They serve as energy conductors to feed our system. Positive awareness opens the portal for energy to flow in the direction of our highest good and greatest joy.

Looking at each chakra's intelligence will show which life issues, qualities, and challenges come under the specific chakras. We can see what negative attitudes do to constrict energy flow, as well as what positive attitudes do to transform our energetic output.

Teaching opens doors to new realms of awareness where unexpressed potential can be developed. Through knowledge, we learn how to negotiate the challenges of life.

Intelligences of the Chakras

Root Chakra: Administrative

Sacral Chakra: Sensation and pleasure

Solar Plexus Chakra: Instinctual knowing

Heart Chakra: Remembering the good

Throat Chakra: Will and expression

Brow Chakra: Control and wisdom

Crown Chakra: Spiritual understanding

Meditation calms and quiets the mind. It allows our small, edited ego to unite with the higher power of self that is always whole, complete, and aware. Through meditation, we connect to our spirit and receive guidance to live an ethical and balanced life.

Opening our minds to the beauty and timelessness of nature can bring peace and a sense of unity with the world.

THE ART OF MEDITATION

Meditation provides a model for you to use when you wish to transform your negative thoughts of unhappiness, hate, or despair. When we find ourselves in unhappy circumstances, or cannot visualize a horizon where we are free from emotional, and sometimes physical, discomfort, it is valuable for us to look within and ask ourselves what we think is the purpose of this situation. What are we learning about ourselves in the face of difficulties? It helps us to put our negativity into a broader perspective and see beyond our self-interest. It helps us regain hope if we are feeling lost.

TRUTH AND INSIGHT

Extricating ourselves from negative situations can take days, weeks, months, and even years. We are blinded to truth and insight. Feelings of loss, betrayal, separation, and anger can overwhelm us. Yet, in telling the truth about our feelings, we yield to their power and learn about ourselves in the process. We also learn that there is something indelible and permanent that is not affected by emotions. This is the self. The self is the substratum of our existence and it never changes, no matter what is happening on the surface of our lives.

EXPLORE YOUR FEELINGS

In looking at a situation that has affected you, ask yourself what your feelings are. Do not judge them. Allow them to be a part of your experience. Ask yourself what is permanent. What is the part of you that is not affected by change? What does that feel like? Did you draw conclusions from this situation? Did you resolve anything in experiencing your feelings? Did you become grounded in the reality of your truth? Can you hold your ground with your awareness?

These aspects of looking at any situation can free you from living in denial or chaos about yourself or a situation. If you trust your feelings and your ability to perceive the truth, you can also make the necessary moves for your health and well-being.

Trust in the source to show you whatever insights you may need to be compassionate, loving, true to yourself, and appropriate with others. Be still and do nothing. Allow the energy you have been holding to be released, and take a moment to be at peace with yourself. Accepting the truth allows you to experience yourself, and this will heal you.

AFFIRMATIONS FOR THE CHAKRAS

- Saying affirmations, such as "I accept myself as I am" and "I love to be loved," is an excellent way of reframing negative attitudes into more positive and life-affirming ones. Stand in front of a mirror and repeat the affirmations again and again.

- When you have integrated the affirmations into your subconscious mind, you may want to record yourself speaking them. Play a tape of your voice at night before you sleep. You can also say them to yourself when you are driving, jogging, or in the shower.

- After you have practiced your affirmations, you can also practice silence. Being quiet stills the mind and helps us value the words we do use even more. In silence, we have an opportunity to listen to angels whispering in our ears. This is how we experience inspiration and guidance.

Decoding your Chakras

When you learn that you can master your own energy field, you find a level of empowerment and vitality that enables you to find and fulfill your life purpose. Understanding your energy system is the first tool to healing what may be out of balance or deficient in your life.

The Root Chakra, MULADHARA, is concerned with keeping life vibrant and sustainable. It incorporates all the qualities to maintain existence in an orderly fashion, including being constant and stable. It is drawn to the simple activity of staying alive. It focuses on shelter, sustenance, and the things that keep our lives moving along. It flourishes with levels of security that keep chaos and evil far from our door, and ultimately it is concerned with having the patience to see our dreams come true.

the ROOT
Chakra

MULADHARA
Root or support

SUPPORT AND SECURITY
Building a structure that supports and sustains our life is a function of the Root Chakra. If our structures are not stable enough to support us, we may become unsure about our right to what we want. Cultivating stability while we form the structure of our life helps us to handle change.

Security is an aspect of the Root Chakra that helps to keep us focused and grounded. When we do not feel secure, we lose energy, fearing for our existence and wondering whether we will go on. Cultivating a deep sense of inner security helps keep the Root Chakra functional during uncertainty.

ANCESTRAL ROOTS

The Root Chakra carries all the qualities
of survival from our ancestors. If our
people fought to maintain a way of life
or to find a better life, their courage and
tenacity are part of our genetic heritage.
Just as the roots of diseases are transmitted
down family lines, so are the spiritual
qualities. When we find ourselves in difficult
circumstances, we can draw on the qualities
our ancestors possessed to see them through.
We can tap into courage, cunning, stealth,
and a ruthless desire to live. It is in our
Root Chakras.

ANCHORING THE SPIRIT

The Root Chakra controls the fight-or-
flight reaction that triggers the adrenal
cortex. This function stimulates the flow
of adrenaline into the blood when we are
under attack, putting us into survival mode.

The Root Chakra anchors itself to the
earth when we are patient, resourceful,
and hopeful about our lives. Remaining
positive and open to possibilities strengthens
the Root Chakra and allows for stability
and inner strength. Anchoring our spirit
in reality is the quintessential quality of
this chakra.

Sage

Qualities and Attributes

Location: In the perineum at
the base of the spine

Age of resonance: Conception
to 7

Sensory experience: Smell

Qualities: Patience, structure,
stability, security, the ability to
manifest your dreams

Life issues: To value the
material as sacred, to find
trust in place of despair,
to persevere

Physical activities: Yoga,
movement of any kind that
activates the legs and feet,
any form of activity that is
grounding, physical, and
demands presence

Spiritual activities: Noticing
the beauty and perfection
of the natural world

Essential oils: Cinnamon,
garlic, sandalwood

Plant: Sage

Metal: Lead

Element: Earth

Musical note: C

Type of music: Drumming

THE ROOT CHAKRA AND THE PHYSICAL BODY

Associated Body Parts
Kidneys, blood, the skeletal system

Physical Problems
Conditions that affect the feet, knees, and hips, including arthritis, kidney stones, osteoporosis, bone problems, and autoimmune deficiency conditions.

Archetypes

POSITIVE:
The Mother

The mother is a person, either male or female, who is nurturing, positive, and hopeful. Mothers encourage, acknowledge, and affirm our being through love, kindness, and absolute faith in the goodness of life. They make the dark moments bearable because they bring us hope of a positive outcome.

NEGATIVE:
The Victim

The victim is a person who, because of external circumstances, is unable to rally regenerative forces and go forward in life. Victims stay alive through the grace and generosity of other agencies, and have little chance of renewing their connection with life as long as they remain dependent upon others to maintain life. They may be temporarily invalided, victims of terrifying circumstances, or completely uprooted from a life they have previously enjoyed.

Glandular Connection: Adrenal Cortex
The cortex is the outer portion of the adrenal gland (the inner portion is called the medulla). The cortex produces corticosteroids that maintain balanced levels of acidity and alkalinity in the cells. It releases amino acids, promotes liver glycogen and glucose formation, and monitors cardiac activity and blood pressure. It controls the flow of adrenaline that fuels our fight-or-flight responses to accidents, stresses, or threats. The adrenaline response can save our lives and keep us actively present in any life-threatening situation. The kidneys themselves contain ancestral vitality and life force. We are dependent on their healthy function to stay anchored in life.

SURVIVAL INSTINCTS

We all face times in life that challenge our resources and try our patience. Few people are taught to be internally resourceful when things go wrong. Developing our resources comes from living life and experiencing change. A healthy Root Chakra is buoyant and flexible. It is adaptable and can remain grounded through changes.

When people become uprooted from their homes and are forced through circumstances to move elsewhere, they will seek a similar condition to the one they know. Imagine a tree that has grown in a certain climate, in specific soil, with fixed amounts of sun, water, and wind. If you uprooted this tree and tried to plant it elsewhere, out of its adaptability zone, it would fail to thrive or would die. People are the same. They need optimal conditions to make successful changes in themselves or their environment.

Even though we are an adaptable and mobile culture when crisis hits, we revert to our basic instincts for survival. Our thoughts turn to shelter, food, water, and warmth. These are fundamental to our lives and come before the realm of comfort, power, love, or ideas.

ASPECTS OF THE SOLAR SYSTEM
Earth and Saturn

ASTROLOGICAL ASSOCIATION
Capricorn

MYTHOLOGICAL ANIMAL

White elephant with seven trunks

EARTHLY LOCATIONS

The Indian preserves and their sacred lands, the sacred lands of all indigenous people

ANGELIC PRESENCE

Archangel Michael, leader of the heavenly armies against the forces of evil

TIMES OF CHANGE

People during times of crisis seek community. They bond with others and reach out in ways previously unknown before they were threatened. Tribal and clan ties sustain people in times of change, and help stabilize the Root Chakra.

During normal times, we are able to turn our attention to developing other qualities. When we find ourselves in new situations under different circumstances, our Root Chakra becomes destabilized and we struggle to maintain both inner and outer equilibrium. At these times it takes only the slightest upset to send us plummeting into despair.

Finding a steady and permanent connection with what is real and true can sustain us through change. Knowing the highest and most eternal truths about the source can sustain us when our grounding is weak and our spirit diminished. Creating a spiritual context in which to place our life experiences is emotionally sustaining.

GENETIC MEMORY

The Root Chakra contains within its structure the underlying attitudes we have about the nature of life. If our ancestors struggled and found life perilous, we will inherit an underlying belief that life is hard and we must struggle. As the Root Chakra is affected by war, pestilence, famine, and chaos, all human beings have some level of dysfunction in their Root Chakras. Few people are truly grounded in a positive and loving sense of life.

All of us have been either uprooted or affected by the hardships of life—if not directly, then through our family history. What our ancestors and family members experienced during hard times is a genetic memory we carry within us. Each time we are stressed or feel threatened, we will react from that place within us where we fear the worst, doubt our chances for survival, and feel that we do not have a right to the life we say we want.

The Root Chakra and the Emotional Body

The Root Chakra is affected by aggression that, if allowed to remain unexpressed, turns into anger and violence. If your life is threatened or your beliefs are attacked, these feelings will stimulate the adrenaline flow into your blood, causing you to become defensive and frightened. Through discovering the emotional charge around you, defending your territory, you open reserves of energy you may never have realized you had, which can be used for creativity and a healthy lifestyle.

It is said that the origins of humanity can be traced to one African woman. This fecund, female energy anchors us deep into the roots of the earth, herself the Great Mother who sustains us.

The Root Chakra and the Mental Body

When our way of life is threatened, the Root Chakra is activated and our ideas become harsh, even hateful in nature. We become defensive and cut off warm feelings to anyone or anything that threatens our home or our institutions. Knowing clearly that we belong in our community and are entitled to preserve our way of life helps us develop tolerance and compassion for strangers and those on the fringe of society.

EXPANDING CONSCIOUSNESS

When we realize that the past has no hold over us, we are free to make our own interpretation of the events in our lives. We are encouraged to try harder, to take a stand for ourselves, and persevere. If the Root Chakra carries too many constrictions and dictates how we feel life needs to be, then we will be pulled down by the weight of tradition, family values, and religious precepts, which will limit and prescribe how we think things need to be. This is neither adaptable nor essential.

We are far more than our family upbringing, our schooling, or our religious beliefs. We are more than our physical body, our emotional stability, and our mental framework about what we think life is. When we expand our consciousness to include the substratum upon which life is based, which is a spiritual consciousness that is eternal, we can be unruffled by the changing tide of events that affect us.

MANIFESTING UNITY

When people live exclusively within the Root Chakra, they are overly attached to land, tradition, home and family, and clan or tribal roots. They do not find their unique individuality or come to express their talents outside the context of these perimeters.

When people exist entirely from their Root Chakras, they are aware only of the petty differences that divide people and nations. They fail to see the bigger picture of one people, one planet. Part of healing the Root Chakra is to eliminate a sense of difference. We open the Root to be an anchor for our spirit and to manifest unity rather than separation.

LIVING CREATIVELY

The archetype of the Root Chakra is the mother. She feeds, nourishes, and provides for our needs. When we honor her, we honor ourselves. Loving and taking care of ourselves is how we become our own good mother. Learning to listen and trust our needs and paying attention to what is good, wholesome, and nourishing for us keeps us grounded. This helps release the negative from our lives and live simply, honestly, and with integrity. Healing our roots is learning that we can do more than our parents did and be more than they were able to be. We broaden our scope and expand our possibilities so that life grows rather than narrows. In essence, we become the best we can be by developing the inner qualities that the Root Chakra stands for, so that we can adapt, make changes, and live creatively.

THE SPIRITUAL DIMENSION

INTELLIGENCE:
Administrative

SOUL LESSON:
Service

The Root Chakra's intelligence helps us to administer our life force. It is based on order in the energetic economy. It is concerned with the qualities of order, security, structure, and stability that we need to make a viable existence. It encourages attitudes that firmly establish our right to the life we say we want. If life has been problematic and full of difficulty, it may be important to investigate the attitudes in your family history that reflect mistrust or encourage expectations of insecurity or despair. We need to cultivate attitudes that trust in the goodness of life through difficult and challenging times. The more inner stability we can mentally create, the more grounded life becomes, and the better we are able to cope with change.

The barn is a symbol of fertility and prosperity, organization and cultivation. It represents structure, stability, and security, as well as a dream manifested. These are all qualities of the Root Chakra.

How to Access the Root Chakra

We can develop viable and healthy Root Chakras when we affirm our right to a good life. This comes when we honor who we are, beyond any limiting identifications that define us by race, age, religion, or nationality. As we affirm ourselves, we strengthen our attachment to life and open the space for it to be fulfilled through us.

The elephant is the mythical animal for the Root Chakra. In India, he is called Ganesha, bringer of good fortune, happiness, and health.

LIFE CHOICES

Each time we define ourselves by the self-limiting ideas that dictate where we can and cannot go, whom we can or cannot participate with, and what we are allowed to do and not do, we narrow our life choices. We define ourselves through race, religion, culture, age, gender, and sexual orientation. We heal our Root Chakra by making choices for ourselves based on the promise of growth and spiritual development.

A RIGHT TO JOY

Our Root Chakra, in order to be functional, must be rid of narrow beliefs. We heal the Root Chakra each time we affirm our right to the life we say we want. Knowing we have a right to joy, happiness, health, and a creative existence is fundamental to life. You need no one's approval, nor do you need reasons to make the choices that promise you happiness, stability, and joy. Stepping away from the prescribed dictates of family, culture, or religion may be painful at first, but eventually your roots become defined by the way you live, love, and communicate, and the choices you make for your life.

Ancient myth says that man was fashioned from clay from the earth, into which God breathed life. Our links to the earth keep our lives simple, creative, and productive.

Negative Attitudes

The negative attitudes associated with the Root Chakra have to do with despair and victimhood. These attitudes can generate violent and hateful feelings. These feelings emerge when our life is threatened and we feel overwhelmed. We may experience such thoughts as "It's not worth it"; "I want to die"; "Life is unbearable this way." They all attest to a malignant disassociation from life and a lack of trust in its innate goodness.

Positive Attitudes

All positive attitudes involving the Root Chakra attest to a spiritual belief in the goodness of life. They imply trust and a sense of belonging, and tell us that there is love, support, and care to get us through difficult and challenging times. It may not come in the form we think we need, but if we are quiet and still we can sense it in nature, in the kindness of strangers, and in many gentle and tender ways. Be still, do nothing. Let the goodness come.

Affirmations for the Root Chakra

Repeat these affirmations once every morning and every evening when you wish to connect with the Root Chakra.

- *I live from my integrity. I love from my heart. I am connected to life in all its glory.*
- *I know who I am and make choices based on what I know to be right for me.*
- *I affirm my right to the life I choose.*
- *I confirm my right to belong and be a part of something greater than myself.*
- *I know I am truly good.*
- *I live from the depths of my soul longing to express itself in the world.*
- *I stand for justice, truth, and love.*
- *I am supported in life through all my choices to do good and share the light of love.*
- *My body supports me in living a creative and happy life.*
- *I am open to the spirit of life that carries me beyond my original limits to a higher, more creative space.*
- *I am thankful for all the opportunities for growth and development that have come my way.*
- *I am grateful for the challenges that have taught me who I truly am.*
- *I love life.*

Meditation for the Root Chakra

Take a few moments to reflect on your early childhood.
Can you identify qualities you possess now that you had then?
Can you see a logical pattern that emerged to make you the person
you are today? If you could offer any guidance to the child that you were,
what would that be? Hold this child in your heart and bless it for
knowing, instinctively, what to do to become the person you are today.

SHAPE
Visualize a large red
cube at the very base
of your spine

VISUALIZATION
When you have done this, take several deep
breaths. Visualize your breath penetrating
to the base of your spine. Each time you
inhale, feel the air you drew in energize
your life force and anchor you in your legs
and feet. Feel your feet connected to the
ground. Visualize a large red cube at the
very base of your spine. Expand the form
and intensify the color. Feel the weight of
this cube anchoring you to the earth. Feel
you are cultivating the qualities of patience,
stability, structure, and security in your life.

REALIZING YOUR DREAMS
You have all the inner resources you need
to make your life work, and the maturity,
stamina, and perseverance to see your
dreams turn into reality. Is there a dream
that you would like to see realized? Can
you see yourself experiencing the reality
of this dream? Allow feelings of fulfillment
to expand your energy field as you bring
your awareness down to the base of your
spine. Once again, expand the form of the

CRYSTALS

RUBY

This precious stone contains the essence of vitality and regenerative forces. A handful of this stone strengthens and revives the heart. It represents the life force in all its power, and is valued for its beauty, fire, and sense of spirit.

BLOODSTONE

This stone is a bright orange-red. It is said to possess the ability to purify the blood. It has a large magnetic field that is believed to heal physical problems, especially those where the blood is stagnant or impure.

HEMATITE

This is a form of magnetic ore with high density. Its silver color attracts the eye and its magnetic qualities make it good for grounding the spirit. Carrying the stone in one's pocket can help keep one's consciousness focused and grounded.

Root Chakra and intensify the color red. Say yes to your dreams. Feel the energy from this large red cube move down your legs, through your feet, and into the ground.

Know that with patience, stability, and a sense of security, your dreams can come true. Affirm your right to life. Say yes to all the trials and tribulations that have brought you to this place of sensitivity and awareness. As difficult as your road may be, are you not grateful for the inner qualities you have developed, the grit it took to achieve the things you truly wanted? Acknowledge the gifts of courage, stamina, and perseverance that you have accessed from your roots.

SEAL THE CHAKRA

Now seal the Root Chakra with a cross of light within a circle of light. Expand the light to include your entire body, the room you are in, the town and country you live in, and the planet itself. Know you are always part of a greater whole and that who you are makes a difference. Take a deep breath as you affirm your being.

Questionnaire on the Root Chakra

The questions for the Root Chakra focus on stability, structure, patience, and security. If you are weak in any particular area, cultivate patience and inwardly create these qualities over a period of time. They can be attained through your conscious awareness of their importance in your life.

THE COLOR OF THE ROOT CHAKRA: RED

Red is the color of the life force. It represents courage, passion, anger, and even violence. It is the color that represents earth energy, anchoring us to the planet that sustains us. It is the most visible color in the entire spectrum and has been used traditionally to signify danger, poison, or threat. The color pulls the retina forward so that our energy is engaged outside of ourselves. It warms, heats, and tones our blood. Too much red can raise blood pressure and create irritation.

Patience

- Do you know how to let things come around in your favor over time?
- Are you addicted to fast fixes and immediate results?
- Are you aware that your impatience is sapping your life energy and burning precious fuel needed for your health and well-being?
- Is impatience or patience a family characteristic?
- Where do your courage, stamina, and grit come from?
- Can you identify family members who were known to have the ability to withstand hardship and change?
- What qualities would you like to develop to help you be more patient with yourself and others?

Structure

- Do you create a life that supports your being the best you can be?
- Do you find fulfillment in the life you have created for yourself?
- To what degree do you need to amend the structures that support your life?
- Can you reflect on a time in your life when you felt supported and upheld?
- What qualities do you need to cultivate in order to build the life you say you want?
- Are you building permanent structures that can help you over the difficult moments in life?
- What do you feel is missing in your support system?

Stability

- How stable do you feel your life is at this moment?
- Are you in need of cultivating higher degrees of internal stability to see you through changes?
- How would you visualize stability? Does it have a feeling or a picture to it?
- Can you recall feeling stable in the past?
- Are you familiar with stability in your history?
- Do you want to cultivate stability in order to realize your dreams about life?
- Being stable means being consistent with your choices for good. Do you bring this into your life?

Security

- How secure do you feel about your life?
- Do you have the basics covered, such as shelter, food, water, and the ability to obtain what you need in times of crisis?
- Do you have a sense of direction about what would give you fulfillment and peace of mind?
- Are you able to withstand changes readily?
- Can you create a sense of security for yourself by knowing that you will be all right no matter what happens around you?
- Can you trust that you are protected and guided as you make your way through life?
- Are you fearful of anything outside your boundaries?

Manifestation

- Do you allow yourself to dream of the life you say you want?
- Do you trust that your greatest joy is possible for you?
- Do you feel that you need to change anything in your life for your dreams to come true?
- Do you feel that you are deserving of what you say you want?
- Can you remain directed doing whatever needs to be done to realize your intentions?
- Are you grateful for the things you have in life now?
- Do you appreciate the dreams that have come true for you in the past?

The Root Chakra is governed by the planet Saturn, which rules time, change, and stability.

WORKING THROUGH NEGATIVITY

- *Cultivate patience, so that when things do not go as planned, you do not lose energy by being frustrated.*
- *Do what is necessary to remain stable through change. Develop meditation skills and ways to slow down the mind.*
- *Learn to live with change. Be flexible and adaptable.*
- *Do not despair when things do not go well for you. Breathe, and give yourself time to reflect on what is essential and important.*
- *Make a plan to see your dreams unfold. Life without a dream is dull.*
- *Enjoy life and cultivate a sense of humor and a positive outlook. We all have setbacks and challenges.*

The Sacral Chakra, Svadhisthana, controls our physical health and well-being. It is the chakra that focuses the life force into building a strong immune system, and keeping the physical body functional and active. It controls our motion and our emotion, and is ruled by the water element that is directly influenced by how we experience our emotions. When we retain our feelings, water is retained in the body. This creates bloating and puffiness, a condition known as idiopathic edema.

the SACRAL Chakra

SVADHISTHANA
My own sweet abode

A BALANCED APPETITE

The essence of the Sacral Chakra is knowing that what we have and do is good enough. This is the center of physical procreation and the chakra directly affecting sexual maturation. It controls our appetites for food, sex, and pleasure. If we are too indulgent, we burn up vital life fuel required by other systems in our body. If we hold back too much energy from the physical part of our lives, we become hungry for what we deny ourselves. Finding the balance between control and letting go is essential for this chakra to function. It takes discipline and maturity to balance this chakra.

SIMPLE NOURISHMENT

The Sacral Chakra is concerned with our physical well-being. This means that we learn to honor the body by giving it what it needs to thrive—nutritious food, plenty of rest, and fun, work, and exercise. This chakra is also concerned with the quality of deservedness. When we feel that we truly deserve the good we long for, we treat ourselves well. We give ourselves permission to have the things we want.

Pleasure is another quality of the Sacral Chakra. It concerns our ability to receive and allow more pleasure into our lives. When we make our lives complex, we strip away the pleasure from our experiences. Finding what is simple can generate joy and pleasure, which nourish the Sacral Chaka.

A healthy Sacral Chakra has defined limits that are neither too open nor too closed. Respecting these limits nourishes the life of the body and lets us know that we are enough for ourselves.

Jasmine

Qualities and Attributes

Location: 2 in. (5 cm) below the navel and 2 in. (5 cm) into the pelvis

Age of resonance: 7–14

Sensory experience: Taste

Qualities: Well-being, sexuality, sensuality, pleasure, abundance

Life issues: To know that who you are and what you do are enough; to have enough rest, food, exercise, fun, and money; not to link self-worth with what you do or have; to create healthy boundaries to protect your vital life force.

Physical activities: Yoga, dance, swimming, walking

Spiritual activities: Meditation, celibacy, fasting

Essential oils: Jasmine, neroli, orange blossom

Plant: Jasmine

Metal: Tin

Element: Water

Musical note: D

Type of music: Latin dance

THE SACRAL CHAKRA AND THE PHYSICAL BODY

Associated Body Parts
Sex organs, bladder, uterus in women, prostate in men

Physical Problems
Dysfunction of the Sacral Chakra in women can create endometriosis, as well as sterility, chronic menstrual cramping, fibroids, and problems with ovaries and cervix. In men, it can create prostate problems, infertility, sexual dysfunction, and sciatica.

Archetypes

POSITIVE:
The Emperor/Empress

The emperor or empress is a person who enjoys and respects the physical world. Emperors and empresses love to have abundance, well-being, and a high degree of pleasure. They know they deserve to feel good about life and enjoy good food, comfort, and some luxury. They are not necessarily spiritual by nature, but they do feel at home on the physical plane and enjoy the good life.

NEGATIVE:
The Martyr

Martyrs deprive themselves of the simple physical pleasures of life. At some basic level, they feel cheated of the goodness of life and punish themselves by forbidding themselves the warmth and comfort they long for. They are full of guilt and project this onto others, making them suffer, too.

Glandular connection: Reproductive Glands
The reproductive glands are the ovaries in women, testes in men; they are governed by the Sacral Chakra and develop by the age the chakra is fully formed at around 14. Their function is to reproduce life and keep the species alive. They develop according to our attitudes about growing into adulthood and being responsible for our sexuality. Problems in this area have a matching counterpart corresponding to our attitudes about sexuality. They are influenced by our relationship to our bodies and how we value our spiritual as well as animal nature. Problems in physical maturation and reproduction are connected to these glands, as well as our attitudes about growing up, having a family, and enjoying our sexuality.

SPIRITUAL VESSEL

This chakra embodies the totality of our physical health and emotional well-being. It can bring us the highest degree of health or be the most dysfunctional of all energy centers in the human energy system. When people abuse their bodies, treating them like machines that need only to be fueled and rested occasionally, they fail to realize that the body is a vessel for the spirit. The Sacral Chakra works from a deep unconscious realm where our attitudes about ourselves create our physical well-being. Our relationship to health, well-being, and joy reflects how much we value ourselves and honor our spirit on the physical plane.

REGENERATIVE ENERGY

The function of this chakra depends on how well we take care of ourselves and know our boundaries and limitations. Proper function ensures that we harness our life force so that we can be creative and spiritual. This chakra promotes regeneration by feeding vital energy into our systems. It stimulates hormonal flow and influences our motility. It controls the way we move and our desire to exercise.

ASPECT OF THE SOLAR SYSTEM
Jupiter

ASTROLOGICAL ASSOCIATIONS
Cancer and Scorpio

EARTHLY LOCATION
Brazil

ANGELIC PRESENCE
Archangel Metatron

MYTHOLOGICAL ANIMAL
A hungry sea monster, waiting to be fed

OPTIMAL HEALTH

We preserve our energy and health by forming wholesome attitudes about optimal health. Finding the right lifestyle, one that encourages physical regeneration, keeps the Sacral Chakra active. Good nutrition is medicine for the body. Keeping the body hydrated and giving it ample rest and time off from stress and pressure keeps us stable and happy. Difficult and challenging experiences strip our bodies of vital energy and deplete our reserves. If this chakra is not replenished, it will drain all other chakras to fill it.

Appreciating the physicality of the body without becoming compulsive or obsessive conserves energy and creates health. It fills the seas of energy reserves that the system can draw from in stressful times. We create these reserves each time we do something good for the body, such as oxygenating our blood with exercise, taking time to smell the roses, and relaxing. Each time we feel good about ourselves and honor our choices, we contribute to our physical presence.

*Svadhisthana means
"my own sweet abode"
in Sanskrit and refers
to the Sacral Chakra,
located in the center
of the pelvis. This
is where pleasure,
deservability, well-being,
and abundance are
anchored in the body.*

ENOUGH IS ENOUGH

The underlying theme of the Sacral Chakra is knowing what is enough. This includes the food we put into our bodies, as well as what we do with our vital energy. Do you dissipate it by giving it away to people and situations that are not pleasurable?

Recuperating from illness or abusive situations requires regenerating the Sacral Chakra. No one returns to health without developing a balanced outlook. If people work too hard and are under constant stress, they leech vitality and well-being from their energy centers. Knowing when to stop, or when something is enough, is a very important boundary for maintaining health.

The important issue is to know that who you are is enough. If someone does not acknowledge you for what you do, the unconscious inclination is to do more to please them. When we know that we are enough, then we make healthy decisions for our well-being.

The Sacral Chakra and the Emotional Body

The Sacral Chakra has a less aggressive emotional response. This is the seat of pleasure and well-being. When we are not experiencing these emotions, frustration builds. When feelings emerge, they are often about what we desire or what we lack. This can be for love, sex, money, and joy. Learning to be grateful for what we have releases much of the frustration or sense of loss held in this chakra. We can learn to sublimate this energy into a balanced lifestyle that is focused on a positive emotional expression of what we have and do.

Sacral Chakra and the Mental Body

The Sacral Chakra harbors attitudes about money, health, deservedness, and pleasure. Sexuality has more constraints around it than any other single issue besides money. How people feel about these subjects has a direct result on their personal energy. When we have harsh ideas about pleasure, we will suffer deprivation and, eventually, disease.

REST AND REGENERATION
Conservation of vitality comes with maturity. Physical regeneration and well-being begin by understanding that what we do and what we have are enough. Taking time out, or a daily rest, giving oneself the space to relax is like applying a preservative. The body heals in sleep and tranquility. Burning up more adrenaline than one needs to creates serious health hazards.

ENERGETIC MEDICINES
If you want health, it is important to know that the body regenerates with the proper stimulus. The body thrives on medicine compatible with one's higher consciousness. Energetic medicines, such as homeopathy, acupuncture, herbalism, and hands-on healing, restore natural vitality. Allopathic medicines give the body heroic doses of chemicals that require large quantities of energy to break down and assimilate. Eating food with additives and diminished life force from radiation and spraying only causes the cells to become stagnant with irritants. All this eventually weakens the body's responses.

DISCIPLINE AND PLEASURE

The Sacral Chakra functions best when there are optimal conditions for joy, relaxation, and pleasure. If the body is used as a beast of burden, it will wear out early and develop painful conditions from the strain. If the body is not given enough stimulation in the form of exercise, it becomes lazy and congested. What is good for the body is good for our energy.

This chakra thrives with a combination of healthy discipline and enough pleasure to ease out stress and tension in the body. It looks for natural solutions that honor the physical being and the spirit of a person. If the Sacral Chakra is looked after properly, the physical body is vital and energetic for well into the senior years. It wears down from a lack of pleasure, harsh and punishing treatment, and physical therapies that do not involve an energetic context for healing.

THE SPIRITUAL DIMENSION

INTELLIGENCE:
Sensation and pleasure

SOUL LESSON:
Peace and wisdom

The Sacral Chakra opens us up to a realm of health, well-being, pleasure, and abundance. If we have attitudes that deny us pleasure, we will live a limited existence. The organism expands with pleasure and contracts with pain. Pleasure helps us sustain a peaceful and joyful life, rich in wisdom about the simple joys of life. The more we develop attitudes that allow us ease, joy, and pleasure, the more energy we have for doing the difficult chores and tasks. Looking at our attitudes about sensuality, sexuality, ease, abundance, and pleasure helps us mature and become our own person. The more we know ourselves, the less we are at the mercy of media marketing designed to make us feel we are somehow lacking. When we know what delights us and gives us joy and peace, then buying something to make us feel "good enough" becomes less attractive.

How to Access the Sacral Chakra

When we honor our physical bodies, we affirm our right to pleasure and well-being. We learn to treat ourselves respectfully by giving ourselves peaceful moments. When we develop a wholesome consciousness about our physicality, we help heal and expand the Sacral Chakra. We also help develop reserves of vitality that can be accessed when we are stressed.

RELEASE TENSION

Giving ourselves space to express our feelings means that we do not have to deal with the consequences of suppressed emotions. What is unexpressed becomes suppressed in the deep musculature of the body, clogging its elasticity and shortening its capacity to extend fully. When we experience those feelings and allow them expression, we help release the body of harmful tension and stress.

JOYFUL LIVING

A wholesome lifestyle invites comfort and ease. It also includes the rigor of a healthy exercise program, along with good nutrition and downtime to relax and have fun. If we have the attitude that we do not deserve pleasure, we miss the opportunities to bring peace and harmony into our existence.

Experiencing a sense of well-being gives us the opportunity to love life more. With a deeper appreciation for life, we become spiritual beings who are grateful to receive the abundance of health, joy, and life itself. When we affirm the joy of living, we project that energy into everything.

Affirmations for the Sacral Chakra

Repeat these affirmations once every morning and once every evening to bring openness to your Sacral Chakra.

- *I love my life.*
- *I honor my body and treat myself respectfully.*
- *I feel the power of healing moving in and through me as I affirm my worth and honor my body.*
- *I trust my feelings and give them ample room for expression.*
- *I lighten my body each time I feel well in myself.*
- *I am a creature of light, open to my highest joy.*
- *I am grateful for the joy of being me.*
- *I receive pleasure and abundance with every breath.*
- *Goodness, beauty, and joy resonate with my soul. I am at one with them.*
- *Healing happens each time I rest, relax, and enjoy myself.*
- *My body responds to thoughts of love and goodness.*
- *I heal any condition that affects me by knowing my body seeks balance and regeneration.*
- *I encourage healing each time I affirm my worth and honor my choices for love.*
- *I love who I am exactly as I am.*
- *There is nothing to change about the way I am. As I love and respect myself, healing happens naturally.*

The crocodile stands for the mythical sea monster that rules the Sacral Chakra. It reminds us that we need food, rest, exercise, and pleasure. When the monster feels deprived of its creature comforts, it becomes irritable and unhappy.

Negative Attitudes

The negative attitudes found in the Sacral Chakra tend to be all about our deservedness of a good life. If we feel we are not worthy of feeling good or of experiencing simple pleasures, we will be unhappy and miserable. We will also make others feel guilty for not making our lives better. These negative attitudes corrode our energy and limit our life force. They instill strict and pious attitudes, while serving to cut us off from ease, joy, and pleasure.

Positive Attitudes

Developing a wholesome outlook toward our body by respecting its need for rest, recreation, touch, and expression helps us transform negative attitudes into healthy ones. Finding the balance between work and ease, prosperity and charity, pushing the body and giving it rest teaches us about wholesome limits. Nurturing the body with tenderness and care creates a possibility for ease and strengthens our right to pleasure.

Meditation for the Sacral Chakra

Begin by imagining the bones of the pelvis acting as a basin for your vital organs and a vital link for the spine and leg joints. See the lower spine coming up through the sacrum and being able to hold the weight of your body. Feel that you are able to carry the burdens of life and still move freely and sensuously. Take several breaths deep into the belly, expanding your lower abdomen. As you release each breath, exhale all tension, negativity, and any sense of disharmony around you.

SHAPE
Imagine a large orange pyramid in your lower abdomen

HEALING PYRAMID
Close your eyes and imagine a large orange pyramid lodged in your lower abdomen. The apex is pointing up toward the heart and the base rests on your hip bones. The four walls of this pyramid represent the qualities of well-being, deservedness, pleasure, and abundance. Expand the form and intensify the color as you create a healing space for your Sacral Chakra to rest in. Keep breathing deeply into your belly, so that tension is released through the breath. See each of the four sides of the chakra becoming upright, strong, and resilient.

STRENGTHENING THE WALLS
The far back wall of the chakra represents well-being. Strengthen it and expand the walls, so that they act as a strong brace against the back of your sacrum. Feel that you have sufficient vitality to move forward in life, doing what you love.

The left-hand wall represents the quality of deservedness. This embraces your right to pleasure, abundance, and good health.

If you have any doubts about what you deserve, release them and trust that life is meant to be pleasurable and comfortable.

Visualize the front wall, which represents pleasure and your capacity for joy. Expand the wall to include your entire pelvis. Whatever negative energy was blocking your capacity for joy is now melting under the warmth and pleasure found in your lower belly. Ease the muscles and breathe deeply. Say yes to life and the goodness around you.

The right-hand wall represents the quality of abundance. Expand your sense of abundance to include all the good things that surround you from the sky, sun, moon, and stars. Be thankful for the beauty of nature. Expand the form of the Sacral Chakra and intensify the color.

Seal the Chakra

Now seal the pyramid with a cross of light within a circle of light. This seals and protects the energy of this chakra. Repeat this meditation on a regular basis to develop a healthy and balanced Sacral Chakra.

CRYSTALS

TIGER'S EYE

This stone is reputed to bring prosperity and abundance. It is a stone that carries good luck and fortune with it, and helps in business and negotiations. Wearing it or keeping it near at hand stimulates physical well-being.

CORNELIAN

This stone, related to the agate family, is the color of the Sacral Chakra. It is meant to promote health and well-being, and bring the wearer pleasure and comfort. It can be found on the shores of oceans and lakes, which suggests its close connection to water and the emotions. It acts to stabilize distraught feelings.

ONYX

This stone has a strong magnetic charge and can stimulate healing at a physical level by magnetizing the blood. When it is combined with a Herkamer diamond, which is a very hard quartz crystal, it creates a powerful energetic force that can be used for healing. It is used to help regenerate and recharge the life force.

Questionnaire on the Sacral Chakra

The following questions are designed to help you place the qualities of the Sacral Chakra into a healthy context. Look at them as an opportunity for you to evaluate what you do with your life energy, and make permanent and sustainable changes that will bring you health and well-being.

THE COLOR OF THE SACRAL CHAKRA: ORANGE

The color of the Sacral Chakra is orange. This is a hot color, full of vital energy and deeply connected with the life force. It represents sensuality and sexuality, as well as a deep connection to joy and passion. This color stimulates physical energy in the body and can open channels of suppressed vitality from an overactive mind. Wearing this color or painting a shade of it in a room brings warmth, healing, and physical well-being. It is the color that affects appetite. Many restaurants and fast-food chains use it to subconsciously increase appetite.

Well-being

- Do you give yourself time off from the grind of daily life? How often in the course of a day do you stop what you are doing and take a break?
- Do you look after your need for nutritious food, enough fluids, vitamin supplements?
- Do you honor your body's need for rest when you are tired?
- Do you give yourself a change of scenery from time to time by going out into nature?
- Do you give your body treatments, such as body work, facials, or massage?
- What do you do to alleviate stress in your body?
- How do you cope with the demands on your time and energy?
- Do you know when to say no to those who are toxic and negative?
- Can you protect your vitality from being drained in wasted conversations and highly dramatic events?

Deservedness

- Do you feel you deserve the life you say you want?
- Do you deserve peace, beauty, and tranquility in your life? Do you deserve love, kindness, and true friends?
- Do you deserve vacations and holidays where you have an opportunity to recharge your vital force?
- Do you feel you deserve to be recognized as a whole person with individual needs?

- Do you feel that you deserve to enjoy life?
- Do you experience dark moments when you feel you are not "enough" and will always be deficient in the things that matter to you in life? Do you feel you deserve to see yourself as "enough"?
- Do you feel that you can manage external pressures knowing that you deserve time out to live your life the way you choose?
- Do you feel you deserve the happiness you long for?

Pleasure

- How much pleasure do you feel you deserve each day? Would you believe that your life can have increased levels of pleasure regularly?
- Do you feel that you can manage to build in pleasure as part of your regular lifestyle?
- To what extent do you try to include joy and pleasure whenever you are planning time for yourself?
- Is pleasure something you trust yourself to enjoy?
- Can you see the joy and pleasure in small things?
- Can you give yourself permission to enjoy what is around you and see the pleasure in looking at the good things in your life?
- Do you complicate your life with too much mental activity?
- Do you overlook the simple and easy way to do things in order to have a big effect on others?

Abundance

- Do you recognize the degree of prosperity you have been blessed with? Are you able to see that abundance in more than the money you have?
- Do you feel that you could manage with less and still feel you had abundance?
- Do you feel you need more money and things to be happy?
- Do you value the things you have now? Are you thankful for the goodness that has sustained you?
- Are you able to create a sense of balance between what you have and what you want?
- Can you relax enough to partake in a celebration of life to give thanks for all you see and enjoy?

WORKING THROUGH NEGATIVITY

- *Honor the physical body by giving it enough food, water, rest, and exercise. Avoid obsessive acts of exertion.*
- *Accept your need for pleasure and create enough good experiences to replenish the spirit as well as the body.*
- *Acknowledge the powerful force of human sexuality and know what your values are regarding it.*
- *Respect the physical world by keeping order, cleanliness, and beauty around you.*
- *Reflect upon the physical energy you put into earning money and the ways that you make financial decisions.*
- *Treat yourself to the joys of life. Know that you deserve what you say you want.*

The Solar Plexus Chakra, MANIPURA, is the center of personal identity. It rules all aspects of our personality and ego, especially our sense of self-worth, self-esteem, and personal identity. This energy center also influences self-confidence, personal power, and freedom of choice. Ultimately, it helps us choose what and who are for our highest good.

the SOLAR PLEXUS Chakra

MANIPURA
Lustrous jewel

EMERGING SELFHOOD
Selfhood emerges during our adolescence and is differentiated by the time we reach young adulthood. The Solar Plexus Chakra regulates an inner knowing and gut instincts about things and people. It develops in relationships, work, finances, and areas of self-management and responsibility. As adults, we are required to establish a personal identity that defines who we are. Facing this challenge, our sense of self begins to emerge. This nurtures the Solar Plexus Chakra and makes it expand. As our sense of self grows, a strong and resilient inner core develops.

Lemon

Qualities and Attributes

Location: Directly below the sternum and over the stomach

Age of resonance: 14–21

Sensory experience: Vision

Qualities: Self-worth, self-esteem, confidence, personal power, freedom of choice

Life issues: To develop a strong and resilient ego, to know you are worthy simply because you exist

Physical activities: Sports, competitive programs, qi gong, hiking, cycling

Spiritual activities: Leadership programs, psychotherapy, amateur dramatics, appreciating solitude

Essential oils: Lemon, grapefruit, juniper

Plant: Carnation

Metals: Iron, gold

Element: Fire

Musical note: E

Type of music: Marches

PERSONAL IDENTITY

Self-worth is the primary quality of the Solar Plexus Chakra. Our personal identity, formed in family life, expands in young adulthood so that we can honor ourselves as we interact and negotiate with the world.

Our true self is that part of us that is always whole and intact. It is where truth, beauty, and freedom abide. It is not affected by pain, loss, or trauma. Though life appears difficult at times, we are made whole when we connect to the self. It is an awareness of invaluable worth, esteem, and true power. The self is more radiant than the sun.

POWER AND RESISTANCE

Personal power also resides in the Solar Plexus Chakra. It forms from developing an abiding sense of who we are. This power can express itself in any situation and guides us through the maze of resistance and opposition placed in our path to help us grow and mature. It thrives in the realm of resistance to form a strong warrior archetype able to stand on its own feet and "fight the good fight." Without challenges that develop inner grit, personal power cannot be developed.

Carnation

THE SOLAR PLEXUS CHAKRA AND THE PHYSICAL BODY

Associated Body Parts
Stomach, liver, gallbladder, pancreas, small intestine, muscles

Physical Problems
Indigestion, acid stomach, ulcers, hepatitis, gallstones, pancreatitis (inflammation of the pancreas), and diabetes.

Glandular Connection: Pancreas
On a physical level, the pancreas controls carbohydrate metabolism, including regulating glucose and insulin in the blood. It also influences nutritional absorption. At an esoteric level, the pancreas is concerned with joy. For instance, diabetes is felt to be a disease of lack of joy and disempowerment. As we develop a sense of selfhood, our level of joy increases and we experience the power of healing in our emotional and physical well-being.

Archetypes

POSITIVE:
The Warrior

The warrior is an empowered person with a definitive sense of selfhood. Warriors know who they are in themselves and in relation to the world. Their sense of self is neither inflated nor weak. They have the inner strength and resilience to see their dreams materialize into reality and the stamina to meet physical and emotional challenges. They are able to fight the good fight for love, victory, and the glory of God.

NEGATIVE:
The Servant

The servant is a person whose sense of personal identity is anchored in the external world, always seeking confirmation from others. Servants work hard for others' acknowledgment. They sabotage themselves by giving their power to others to define who they are and what they need to do. They lose energy trying to please others for the affirmation they are unable to give to themselves.

THE IMPORTANCE OF DUALITY

The shining light of selfhood reflected in
the Solar Plexus Chakra requires that we
see the world in a state of duality. This
means that there has to be opposition and
contradiction to rub against in order for our
internal development to take place. From
the view of this chakra, we will witness life
in terms of "us and them" or "others." This
duality is how the ego is formed and how
it cultivates a sense of itself in the world.

INDIVIDUALITY

This chakra is the center of our ego, which
is our individuality, and the ego always
perceives life in terms of duality, frontiers,
and boundaries. The Solar Plexus Chakra
develops as we formulate our personality
and sense of individuality. Without
challenges to create a strong internal sense
of life, we stagnate and fail to mature. The
Solar Plexus Chakra governs the ages from
14 to 21. It culminates at the time when
young people begin their path in life. Some
opt for marriage or other love relationships,
others take on jobs or start careers. All
face entering the world, engaging in
relationships, and developing selfhood.

ASPECTS OF THE SOLAR SYSTEM
Mars and the sun

ASTROLOGICAL ASSOCIATIONS
Aries and Leo

EARTHLY LOCATION

United States of America

ANGELIC PRESENCE

Archangel Uriel,
regent of the sun

MYTHOLOGICAL ANIMAL

Lion

CONFIDENCE

Young adulthood and all new beginnings are governed by this chakra. At this time of life, it is appropriate to make mistakes as well as wholesome choices. Each challenge faced helps develop other internal qualities that define selfhood. Confidence and self-worth, as well as personal power, come from meeting the world on your own terms.

These qualities are a natural outflow of the choices we make for ourselves. In young adulthood, we learn from trial and error and develop confidence in our ability to stand on our own. Character formation does not come because of our family, our connections, or what we perceive to be our right; it comes out of experience of knowing who we are.

The first three chakras—Root, Sacral, and Solar Plexus—are concerned with family, tribe, clan, and country. They help us individuate and find our sense of personal identity.

The Solar Plexus Chakra and the Emotional Body

The Solar Plexus Chakra's emotions revolve around power. They reflect our relationship to inner strength and self-worth. These emotions help us take a stand for ourselves. If we are comfortable with our power, we will act confidently and exercise freedom of choice in most matters. If we are uncertain and doubtful about our right to our own power, we will evade situations that call for an affirmative response.

PERSONAL POWER

Personal power is the ability to influence others and make changes in any situation. It comes from having done something well with impeccable integrity. When we realize the discipline we put into making things happen in our lives, we choose a path to mastery and the cultivation of personal power. Each time we finish a task, complete a course of action, or stand by someone when the odds are down, we add depth and quality to our personal power. These are all the qualities that define character.

FREEDOM OF CHOICE

Freedom of choice is the ultimate determination of the Solar Plexus Chakra. The choice to be ourselves, to choose love, respect, and kindness, and to do what we know is right is something that every generation has sacrificed to maintain. We make good decisions for ourselves when we know our worth, have a sense of pride in our efforts, and feel confident about our abilities. This is how personal power comes about. When all these components are in place, we are able to make wholesome choices that enhance freedom. This is one of the most essential aspects of humanity that we cherish and value.

Instinct is common to all life forms. Our instinctual knowledge is linked to the Solar Plexus. It allows us to be aware of our deep-felt, gut reactions to situations and people. Honoring these feelings is both self-protective and necessary for spiritual self-preservation.

The Solar Plexus Chakra and the Mental Body

The Solar Plexus Chakra holds thoughts about power, confidence, and freedom of choice. If we fail to value ourselves, our ideas about power may be inflated or deflated, depending on how we see ourselves in relation to others. When we know who we are, we cultivate power carefully and cherish our freedom to choose what is right for us.

MAINTAINING A HEALTHY EGO

The Solar Plexus Chakra extends into the realms of the heart. It influences the way we respond to situations through compassion and love. It is especially connected to the heart by how strongly we love and value ourselves. If we are disconnected from our heart, we run the risk of becoming manipulative, exploitative, and egotistical. Keeping checks on the ego so that it is connected to the self is both healthy and mature. When the ego gets too strong, a high degree of separation exists between oneself and another, and others are regarded as objects.

The Solar Plexus resonates at the time we begin our path into adulthood. Our sense of self is intact and we begin to know what we wish to pursue in life.

DEVELOPING SELFHOOD

Gut instincts are centered in this chakra. How we respond to external influences shows how strong our warrior archetype is. When we act from a place of strength, able to take control of our lives, and embody heroic qualities that instill confidence and trust in others, we gain power and the ability to influence situations and people. When fear dominates our lives, we lose energy and power and create dependency on others for our well-being.

We have the capacity to heal others as well as ourselves by developing selfhood. This requires formulating a healthy and wholesome personality able to stand on its own. It requires knowing who we really are at the core and making wholesome choices from a place of optimal freedom. Allowing the Solar Plexus Chakra to be all it can be means that we allow ourselves to be the same.

THE SPIRITUAL DIMENSION

INTELLIGENCE:
Instinctual knowing

SOUL LESSON:
Human and divine love

The Solar Plexus Chakra quickens when we anchor our personal identity in the abiding nature of the self. This challenges the external labels we use to identify ourselves that limit who we truly are. If we are identified with being a certain way and we maintain a specific image that people can approve, respect, or accept, we live a life based upon maintaining that image and avoid dealing with our spiritual nature, our true self. Forming wholesome attitudes around selfhood, freedom of choice, personal power, and confidence stems from connecting with our innate sense of worth. We are value itself, and there is nothing we need do to prove our worth. Once we realize we are worthy, simply because we exist, we free our life force and liberate energy for living.

The Solar Plexus Chakra is the center for personal empowerment. When we accept ourselves and know that we are worthy of love and respect, we feel at peace and generate peace around us.

How to Access the Solar Plexus Chakra

As the center for personal empowerment, the Solar Plexus Chakra can be mastered only when we know our worth and connect to the world through an abiding sense of self. When the ego has a healthy link to the self, it negotiates with the world in a balanced and considerate way. It is neither inflated nor manipulative or exploitative.

Fire is the element that rules the Solar Plexus Chakra. This is named for the sun and is the center of our sense of personal identity. As the physical body uses this chakra to break down food into usable nutrients using heat, so the lower mental body found in the Solar Plexus breaks down ideas for us to assimilate mentally for our growth and development.

PERSONAL IDENTITY

When our personal identity is intact, we know who we are. We know we are worthy of love, kindness, and respect, and that the world mirrors this sense of worth back to us in relationships, jobs, and our daily lives. People who do not know who they are act out of a need for recognition and attention. Instead of generating peace and harmony, they often create drama and chaos.

POSITIVE CHOICES

When this chakra is activated and balanced, we make positive choices for our lives. As we grow and develop a strong and resilient ego, we build reserves of energy that we can draw on when we are tired, ill, or distressed. We learn to trust our instincts so that we can differentiate between what and who are and are not really good for us.

The nature of the Solar Plexus Chakra is power itself. If power is too strong, this chakra becomes manipulative. When it is deflated, people lose the grit to get through challenging situations. In accessing this chakra, we learn to deal with issues of power and turn them positive situations.

Affirmations for the Solar Plexus Chakra

Repeat these affirmations once every morning and once every evening to strengthen your Solar Plexus Chakra.

- *I am worth my weight in gold.*
- *I am worthy of love, kindness, and respect, regardless of what I have done.*
- *I am worthy because I exist.*
- *I am worthy of the life I say I want.*
- *I am worthy of the best.*
- *I am confident in my ability to make my life work.*
- *I am confident in the goodness of life itself to see me through.*
- *I accept the power of my being to produce health, love, and joy in my life.*
- *I know I am a powerful and wholesome force for good.*
- *I choose the power of life.*
- *I choose goodness, light, and love.*
- *I choose health, healing, and happiness.*
- *I choose the best for myself.*

Knowing that you are worth your weight in gold may help you realize that you are worthy of love, kindness, and respect.

When we take responsibility for our feelings of anger or joy, we know that we are entitled to them and we reclaim both confidence and power.

Negative Attitudes

Any time we deny our essential worth, we give away our power and deplete this chakra. The foundation of the Solar Plexus Chakra is an acceptance of our intrinsic value as a person with individual rights. These concern respect for and the worth of our being. Whether or not things are going well does not affect our sense of worth. It is not negotiable, nor is it determined by external events. Negative attitudes that deny our selfhood deprive us of love, kindness, and respect. They diminish us by letting us be manipulated and exploited.

Positive Attitudes

Honoring the self allows a wealth of respect, kindness, and goodness to come our way. When we acknowledge the wealth of our being, we will seek out situations and people who honor us as individuals and affirm our worth. Cultivating a sense of worth may feel unfamiliar at first. Begin by making small, incremental shifts in how you perceive yourself. Allow the truth of your experience to keep you balanced, so that you become neither inflated nor deflated.

Meditation for the Solar Plexus Chakra

Take several large and deep breaths, as though into your stomach, and exhale slowly and completely before resuming another breath. Do this six times before continuing. This area accumulates tension and is often painful and tight in many people. You can rub the abdominal area with your fingers to loosen it as you do this breathing exercise. When you feel relaxed, close your eyes and begin the meditation.

SHAPE
Visualize a large golden globe that expands out from your belly

GLOBE OF LIGHT
Begin by visualizing a large golden globe that expands out from your belly. Allow this globe to fill your entire abdomen. See the golden light warming you and releasing tension in your stomach, gallbladder, liver, and pancreas. This light reaches into the dark corners of your organs, filling each recess with light. It helps you to relax even more as tension is released with each breath.

Breathe deeply into your body and feel the warmth of your own light take away the stress and pressures you have recently experienced. Know that you are worthy of the life you say you want. Love, prosperity, and goodness are possible for you. Begin to experience confidence in your ability to meet the challenges of your life.

CHOOSE EXCELLENCE
You have the power to see things through to a positive conclusion. Choose to do the best you can. Choose love, light, and healing in all aspects of your life. Allow this light to move in and through you and shine in front

of you as you experience your intelligence and love for freedom. If you feel confused, frightened, or weak, be assured that you can master your fears and put chaos behind you. By accepting your spiritual lessons within your surroundings, you will find the power to change your life.

The Solar Plexus Chakra moves us to excellence, just as living tends to cultivate our character. When our physical, emotional, and mental health is challenged, time should be taken to firm up our footing. Know that it is our intentions that allow us to achieve what our heart desires. Be flexible, compassionate, and open to changes. A new approach can be revealed to us unexpectedly at any time.

SEAL THE CHAKRA

When you have expanded the form of the Solar Plexus Chakra, visualize a cross of light within a circle of light. Whenever you feel too diffuse, spaced out, or frightened, visualize this large golden globe in your solar plexus and seal it with a cross of light within a circle of light. It will give you protection, grounding, and a sense of yourself at all times.

CRYSTALS

TOPAZ

This has been the traditional stone of courage and healing. It was found in the breastplate of the high priest Aaron, mentioned in Exodus. It denotes instinctual understanding of life issues and challenges. It brings healing by giving us confidence in ourselves.

AMBER

This is a crystallized resin. It is believed that the sap came from ancient trees that were alive during the Matriarchy, the time in which women held reign over the practicalities of life, and were the priests and driving force in the culture. This happened between 15,000 and 750,000 years ago according to some sources. Amber is associated with feminine power and is thought to be a stone for women finding their internal empowerment.

CITRINE

This stone combines the yellow found in the Solar Plexus and the green in the Heart Chakra. It is the color of spring shoots and suggests transition, new beginnings, and an awakening of the heart. It is used to stabilize love of oneself by honoring our personal choices for growth and spirituality.

Questionnaire on the Solar Plexus Chakra

The questions concerning the Solar Plexus Chakra are divided into the qualities that govern this center. Work to develop these qualities if they are weak. They will help generate a strong sense of selfhood that will give you strength in challenging situations.

THE COLOR OF THE SOLAR PLEXUS CHAKRA: YELLOW

Yellow contains more light than any color in the visible spectrum. It is associated with the sun and the metal gold. It is a diffuse color that creates confusion with overexposure. Because there is so much light in yellow, one can become disoriented as well as cheered. Yellow is a warm color that gives off heat, though less intensely than orange or red. It lifts the spirit and gives hope, as well as a sense of ease and lightness. Yellow is associated with fire energy that can break down other elements. We need this color to create a proper mental framework, so that we can digest new ideas.

Self-worth

• How strongly do you value yourself?
• Do you know the ultimate worth of selfhood?
• Do you honor your sense of who you are in situations with family and friends?
• Do you hide your innate sense of worth from others because you think you will be different?
• Do you see worth in others when they do not see their own light shining?
• Can you connect within yourself to this place of light, intelligence, and love?
• Are you willing to take the time and do the inner work to cultivate a strong anchor to your selfhood?

Self-esteem

• What things are you the most proud of having done in your life?
• Do you feel that you can value past achievements?
• Do you respect yourself for having done a good job at certain things in life?
• What do you consider to be the kindest thing you have ever done?
• Are you willing to acknowledge yourself for being able to see something through to its conclusion, especially if it was difficult and challenging?
• What are the consequences of your having put yourself on the line to accomplish a task?
• Do you value your ability to do good?

Confidence

- Are you confident in your ability to do something well?
- Are you pleased by the way you can choose to do a project and complete it?
- Are you confident in your ability to make necessary changes in your life?
- Are you confident that you see a good opportunity when it presents itself to you?
- Are you confident in your ability to communicate your needs to those around you and be understood?
- Are you confident in your ability to make good choices for yourself in relationships?
- Are you confident that you will succeed in your tasks and with things that are important to you?

Personal power

- Are you willing to express yourself in a powerful way that lets others know not to mess with you?
- Are you able to use your personal power to do something that makes life better for others?
- Are you clear about your need to balance your personal power with humility and compassion?
- Do you abuse your personal power by being difficult with those not in a position to challenge you?
- Do you cultivate your personal power and learn to temper it when appropriate?
- Do you honor your power by using it only when necessary?

Freedom of choice

- Do you know that you are always free to choose in every situation?
- Do you exercise your freedom to choose to be yourself at all times?
- Do you honor this gift and defend it when asked to make a decision?
- Do you realize that freedom of choice is essential to your human development?
- Do you prize this gift above all others?
- Do you experience freedom when you make a choice for the good in your life?

WORKING THROUGH NEGATIVITY

- *Develop a sense of your own person. Know that who you are is always the same, even in a variety of circumstances.*
- *Create your own sense of personality that lets others know who you are.*
- *Following the crowd may be safe, but it will always be limiting and stultifying.*
- *Spend time alone with yourself. Learn to cultivate your own friendship.*
- *Ask yourself if you are worthy of the life you say you want.*
- *Find out where your talents and gifts lie.*
- *Do not be afraid to try new things. Experience of self develops from placing yourself in challenging situations.*
- *Travel and exploration help define you in the face of adversity and challenge.*
- *Learn to recognize character and integrity in yourself and others.*

The Heart Chakra, ANAHATA, governs the physical heart and lungs. It is the center of the human energy system. The Heart Chakra functions both physically and emotionally to keep the life force alive. Just as the heart organ carries the life blood through the body, so the Heart Chakra moves love through our lives. The heart thrives on brotherhood, joy, peace, and understanding. A happy heart is a tonic of life. Gradually, we mature and need to take less. Instead, we give love unconditionally.

the HEART
Chakra

ANAHATA
Unstruck

LOVING NATURE

The Heart Chakra operates on the physical as well as the emotional and energetic planes. It is essential to our physical supply of energy and vitality, as well as the love that nourishes our spiritual existence. Centering ourselves in love gives our life purpose and meaning. It anchors us in selfhood, which is love itself. What this means, on a real level, is that our nature is loving, kind, and respectful. Growth and healing open a panorama, where we give love freely and unconditionally and receive it in the same way.

Qualities and Attributes

Location: Middle of the chest

Age of resonance: 28–35

Sensory experience: Touch

Qualities: Unity, brotherhood/sisterhood, love, peace, purity, innocence

Life issue: To let love be the center of your life

Physical activities: Yoga, massage, healing touch, walking, dancing

Spiritual activities: Learning to love yourself first, then others, prayer, healing, singing, joyful endeavor

Essential oils: Rose, carnation, lily of the valley

Plants: Foxglove, rose, carnation, lily

Metals: Copper, gold

Element: Air

Musical note: F

Type of music: Choral

EXPANSION AND JOY

The Heart Chakra is partially open in early childhood, and closes down as we mature and become products of our culture. If there was a lack of love in the beginning of life, it can be difficult to allow the heart to open. At some point in early adulthood, around age 28, the Heart Chakra seeks to expand, longing for love. It searches for ways in which it can open. Certain experiences trigger this blossoming: relationships forged, children born, choices made that let us love ourselves better. At this age, the heart is ready to engage in real and mature love, for the self and others. Not to allow this natural evolution obstructs normal development.

The pull of sex, power, and money pales in comparison with the joys of the heart. Love is something that stays in our hearts forever. Being willing to experience lasting love, rather than indulge in temporary attractions, is the significance of the Heart Chakra.

Rose

The Heart Chakra is the energy center that unites couples and brings emotional healing.

Archetypes

POSITIVE:
The Lover

This is a person whose ground of being is centered in the heart. They love unconditionally, and heal the tight, hard places in those they touch because they bring warmth and acceptance. They generate goodness and are genuinely embracing and kind. Their love is inclusive, uniting those on the outside. They share love with everyone. They know that to love is to live. Knowing this archetype changes your life for the good.

NEGATIVE:
The Actor/Actress

This is a person whose love is conditional. They have expectations about how and whom they can love. If someone falls outside the realm of their conditions, they withhold their love. They love in the limited way they have been loved, with judgment and criticism for what does not fit into their framework. They love through imitation rather than true feeling. Their relationships often dry up because they have not developed a capacity to hold love in their hearts.

THE HEART CHAKRA AND THE PHYSICAL BODY

Associated Body Parts
Pericardium, heart, lungs, circulation

Physical Problems
Arteriosclerosis, angina, myocardial infarction, heart arrhythmia, stenosis of the heart and lungs, pneumonia, chronic bronchitis, and tuberculosis.

Glandular connection: Thymus

This gland is found in the upper chest. It serves as an important component in preserving immunity. The thymus gland also has a relationship to our emotional well-being. When we are happy and expressing love in our lives, it functions well, secreting hormones that tone the heart and keep the lungs active. When we are not happy, the thymus becomes underactive. It fails to thrive. Energy from the Heart Chakra nourishes this gland. Living in a state of joy, finding people, things, and activities that make your heart sing, keeps the thymus healthy. Thymus extract or homeopathic preparations can be used whenever there has been loss, rejection, or painful emotional trauma. It keeps the immune system balanced.

SACRED CONNECTION

The qualities of the Heart Chakra are peace, love, unity, brotherhood and sisterhood, and joy. All these aspects of the heart speak of love of life and a penetrating awareness of the sacredness of all things. The heart thrives on joy and delight; it flourishes on openness, sharing, touch, and connection. It contracts with pain, loss, and trauma. Feeding the heart with positive energy is choosing to see the love in people, and the joy in all things.

The message of the Heart Chakra is to accept the oneness of all life. Through loving, we radiate the joy of being. An open Heart Chakra is experienced by others as warm, inviting, and tender. An old Irish saying goes, "Find people who warm you." This refers to seeking a true heart connection with others.

ASPECTS OF THE SOLAR SYSTEM
Venus and the sun

ASTROLOGICAL ASSOCIATIONS
Libra and Taurus

**EARTHLY
LOCATION**

Spain

**ANGELIC
PRESENCE**

Archangel Raphael

**MYTHOLOGICAL
ANIMAL**

Deer

UNITY AND BELONGING

Deep healing comes through the Heart Chakra. This is where, according to mystics, God lives within each of us. Our heart song resonates with the pulse of our being. As we evolve, we long for a heart connection in all things. It gives us a sense of unity and belonging; it helps us share the best of ourselves with others.

The heart suffers whenever there is a sense of separation or isolation. For the heart to heal, we employ forgiveness, prayer, meditation, and positive intent to release old hurts that weigh us down and perpetuate the illusion of our singularity.

LOVE FOR ONESELF

Once we transcend the lower chakras and come into the realm of the heart, there is only oneness. Power, sex, and money no longer hold a thrill or sustain our feelings. Joy comes when we are connected to love, unity, and peace. Removing impediments to the experience of love takes love itself, especially for oneself. This love may take the form of seeking help from a teacher, therapist, or friend. It implies it is time to fill the heart with love and release any sense of inferiority, unworthiness, and lack.

Getting to the core of the heart means becoming aware that who we are and what we do are love itself. There is no divisibility here. In the realm of heart, we are connected to the divine heart.

DIVINE GRACE

A strong heart is able to forgive the wounds of the past, find joy in the moment, and step into the world to make it a better place. Our path toward love keeps us light, positive, and open to our highest good. The great Satguru, Sri H.W.L. Poonja, says our spiritual challenge is to love the self and have the heart of a lion through the thick and thin of life. As we gracefully surrender to life, we allow it to move us, and with an open heart we accept ourselves and others in divine grace.

RECEPTIVE TO LOVE

The heart never forgets acts of kindness, friendship, or love. Being loved, accepted, and nourished is how we manage to go forward in life. If we do not receive this from an external source, our growth process is to learn to give it to ourselves. When the mind chooses to dwell on the negative, the heart is leeched of what it needs to survive. It only wants to remember the good and the joyful and feel love in the present moment.

The mind, by its very nature, is divisive and creates the illusion of duality. The heart unifies, and brings together the threads of love, whether from those closest to us or the kindness of strangers. The heart's work is to be receptive and allow love to be.

The Heart Chakra and the Emotional Body

The Heart Chakra is the center of love. It opens us to experience love for ourselves and others. It lets us feel compassion, joy, and peace. As the heart expresses love, it permeates all aspects of our life and enriches our relationships. The heart is the essence of joy.

We may not have been consciously aware of the love that was shown to us when we were younger, but love experienced stays in our soul forever.

Nourish the heart by spending time in nature. She is the supreme healer, giving us the space to breathe clean air, and find tranquility and beauty.

The Heart Chakra and the Mental Body

The Heart Chakra holds ideas and attitudes about our worthiness to give and receive love. The more we love ourselves and accept the wounds of human fragility, the more we begin to love others. The heart is the seat of joy. We bring healing to the heart when we allow life to be joyful and loving. Learning to place one's love in the sacred vault of another's heart allows the heart to be full. The heart longs to trust in love.

KEEPING AN OPEN HEART

The heart is nourished by peace and is kept happy and stable. It is important to nourish the heart by spending time in silence, in nature, and with positive people. It helps to read uplifting books and to cultivate laughter and play in one's life. Doing what makes your heart sing keeps the heart strong and alive. An open heart receives as much as it gives.

We revive a wounded heart by our ability to see the good, and forgive the past. This helps us regain energy that has gone into suppressed feelings. Each step toward reconciliation with our self helps release vitality that we can use for creative living. Reconciliation means forgiving the past and living in the present.

HEART PROTECTOR

The Heart Chakra is made up of two distinct components. The first is the heart protector. This corresponds to the pericardium (a double-walled sac that surrounds the heart) and acts to protect the heart from external assault. It keeps unwanted criticism, negative thoughts, and impure intentions away from the purity and innocence of the heart.

We forge a strong heart protector by developing an uncompromising love of self that is reflected in healthy boundaries, and knowing who and what are for our highest good. Our hearts are nourished by love of nature, animals, children, and the elderly. Loving our lives, loving others, and sharing this light heals us and heals the world.

THE JEWEL WITHIN

The second component to the Heart Chakra is the heart itself. It is pure, innocent, and unblemished. It is the eternal abode of the Holy Spirit in each individual. Knowing the depth, purity, and beauty each individual has been graced with in life can only make us mindful of the jewel that rests in each person's heart. Awakening the connection to that place of love and purity takes love and trust in God, however one chooses to define the infinite intelligence that guides our spirit. Seeking that outside of ourselves will only lead us back to where we have started our search, within our own heart.

THE SPIRITUAL DIMENSION

INTELLIGENCE:
Remembering the good

SOUL LESSON:
Brotherhood and love

The Heart Chakra's attitudes are based on love, compassion, and healing. Developing an open Heart Chakra comes from knowing that we are love itself. As we mature and require less sustenance from the external world to nurture us, we become better able to give out love, warmth, and healing from a kind and generous spirit. When we cultivate attitudes based on our right to love and be loved, wounds rooted in anger and loss can be healed. The Heart Chakra's need to love is its only driving force. It can be happy loving animals, nature, or the world at large. It thrives on the two-way nature of relationships so that it can function with peace, warmth, care, and a sense of oneness. Allowing the heart to do its job is what the body/mind/spirit continuum is all about.

Joy comes when we are connected to another. Love feeds us, heals us, and lets us know that its fulfillment is our highest purpose on this earth.

How to Access the Heart Chakra

Mending the heart so that it is able to love again is the basis of all healing. We all need love as the essential core of our lives, and, if painful wounds have closed the heart off from receiving, it is essential to revive it. The realization that we are love helps ease the pain of rejection or loss. Developing compassion for those who are not able to love us in the way we desire is the awareness of an awakened heart.

We learn love, in its purest sense, from the archetypes of history and religion. The Madonna and Child are the symbol of divine love made flesh. They imply purity of heart and innocence.

LOVE YOURSELF

Spiritual enlightenment is the awareness that we are love. What we seek in the external world is a mere reflection of our true nature. When we know we are love, then love finds its way into our lives. When we release dark feelings that block the Heart Chakra, we open the channel for love to find us. One of the primary principles of healing is first to love ourselves. We do more to mend our wounded heart by accepting our own love and the recognition of wholeness. From that point, we are free to love others and cultivate good relationships.

UNCONDITIONAL LOVE

We are all entitled to the love we say we want. If we feel a need to limit love by placing conditions on it and controlling the way in which it comes to us, we will never know the thrill of experiencing a deep love. It comes from nature, plants, animals, and the world around us. In fact, it is everywhere; we only need to open our hearts to feel it. By its very nature, love is unlimited, unconditional, and free.

Affirmations for the Heart Chakra

Repeat these affirmations once every morning and once every evening when you wish to access your Heart Chakra.

- *All love resides within my heart.*
- *I am quiet and listen to my heart's song.*
- *I choose to be united with all beings, visible and invisible, in the realm of love and light.*
- *I anchor my heart in truth, love, and God's grace.*
- *Love opens and heals me.*
- *I choose the peace that surpasses all understanding.*
- *I am love, I am peace, I am light.*
- *I follow my heart's desire for truth and goodness and love.*
- *My core is pure and innocent. Nothing can touch the soul of my heart except love itself.*
- *God's love fills me and opens my heart to all goodness.*
- *Joy is my reason for living.*
- *I look for the joy in myself and see it in all things.*
- *I delight in sharing my joy.*
- *I let my heart shine and give from the depths of my being to those who accept love.*

Mother's love is the first unconditional loving experience we have in life. It is the strongest bond we experience until we find someone in our adult life who offers us companionship, trust, and sharing.

Negative Attitudes

The fear of giving and receiving love blocks health, joy, and goodness from coming into our lives. Fear is the opposite of love. It prevents the heart from being happy and joyful and corrodes the spirit. Avoiding doing what delights us and suffering over loss weakens the heart. Failing to do what we love deprives the heart of its main purpose, which is to love.

Positive Attitudes

Allowing love to be the core of our life carries us through difficult and challenging times. It keeps our spirit open and our heart alive. Loving who we are, what we do, and how things are raises the spirit and heals the heart. Knowing that we are love is part of the very fiber of our being. It helps us create a positive, generous attitude toward others and heals wounds of pain, loss, or separation. Love is the greatest gift we can give ourselves. It makes us whole.

Meditation for the Heart Chakra

Meditating on the Heart Chakra is done in two parts. First, we experience the nature of the heart protector. Its qualities are love, joy, unity, fraternity, and peace. They can act as an invincible shield against the challenges we face in life. The second part of this meditation focuses on the heart itself, which is always pure and innocent. Taking time to feel the depth of your heart will open your connection to the spiritual realm.

SHAPE
Visualize a green crescent moon across your upper chest

VISUALIZE THE HEART PROTECTOR
Sit comfortably with your back straight. Take several deep breaths and begin to relax. Let your jaw be free and loose, and let your tongue relax in your mouth. Let your eyes relax and move deeper into your skull. If you feel any tension, breathe into that area of your body and tell it to relax.

When you are at ease, begin to visualize a green crescent moon that goes across your upper chest from shoulder blade to shoulder blade. Expand the form and intensify the color. This is the heart protector that provides a safe haven for the pure and gentle spirit of the heart. You can inflate this protector by strengthening your sense of love, peace, unity, and brotherhood, and feeling your joy.

HEALING WITH NATURE
Visualize a scene in nature where you are surrounded by beauty. Keep your attention here until you feel ready to move on. Enjoy the peace and healing that nature gives us

with her beauty. As you hold this vision, feel safe and protected from harm. Feel your heart, which you can visualize as either pink or gold, and let it expand as its energy fills your entire being with grace. You may experience a lightness of being and a sense of resiliency, and a knowing that you have enough love in you to heal the entire world.

GOD'S DWELLING PLACE

The heart is the cave where God dwells within you. You may rest quietly in knowing that this connection is always with you. Know that you are loved, guided, and protected at all times. You can gently leave your ego at the door of this cave and let your consciousness enter within its confines. As you step inside, see the diamond of your self brilliantly lighting up the inside of your heart. This diamond represents the light of your self, that part of you that is eternal and is the heart of God within you. As you honor that, know that you are always connected to this place within.

SEAL THE CHAKRA

As you come out of your meditation, be sure to seal the Heart Chakra with a cross of light within a circle of light. This seals in the energy of the heart space and allows it to bring you healing. Take your time coming back into your waking reality. Look at yourself in the mirror and acknowledge that you are the love you feel. Take your gentleness out into the world and let it be reflected back at you.

CRYSTALS

ROSE QUARTZ

This is a semiprecious stone that stands for love. It is found to resonate with the energy of the Heart Chakra. Its color soothes tension in the heart and brings the vibration of love to all who wear it or keep it near them. Used in a room, it keeps the energy loving and kind.

DIAMOND

This most precious of all gemstones stands for fidelity, loyalty, and divine love. It represents the truth of God's eternal love and is used in wedding rings to signify eternal, undying love, and commitment.

PERIDOT

This semiprecious stone contains the energy of young spring shoots. It mixes the sense of selfhood found in yellow with the balance, tranquility, and unity of green. It brings healing to a fragmented personal identity and stimulates confidence and love of self.

Questionnaire on the Heart Chakra

These questions are meant to assist you to see the love in your life.
Be gentle with yourself as you look at these questions. Allow love to
flow as a constant factor in your relationships with people. Even if your
love is not actively received, it is not lost. Love and caring intentions
are always influencing others, so bless the past and set it free.

THE COLORS OF THE HEART CHAKRA: GREEN AND PINK

Green is the color that brings balance, peace, and tranquility, soothing the nerves and acting as a tonic when we are weary or depressed. Nature gives us her healing power through this color more than any other. Monks making copied illuminations used to hold green beryl up to their eyes to relieve eye strain. Pink is the color of mother love and is found in the aura of all babies and young children. Pink is soft, sweet, and soothing. Pink lifts the emotions, purifies the spirit, and generates a tender quality, suggesting approachability.

Love

- Do you feel love for yourself and for others in your life?
- Do you feel love for the beauty of nature and animal life around you?
- Do you feel love for life in general?
- What makes your heart sing and gives you joy?
- Do you love sharing the things that you care about?
- Can you offer up your love to the world around you?
- Can you remember the people in your life you deeply loved?
- Can you forgive those who hurt you in the past?

Peace

- How much peace do you create in your life?
- Do you have peace of mind? Place?
- Do you need to fill your life with experiences and people who are not peaceful?
- What gives you a sense of peace? Is it music? Nature? Quiet? Painting?
- How important is peace in your personal life? In your professional life?
- What can you do to ensure that you have peace?
- Do you long for peace and feel it is elusive?
- Do you need to make changes in your life that will allow more peace in?

Brotherhood/sisterhood

- Do you believe that we are all connected?
- Do you see the people around you as your equals?
- Do you see through the social and cultural constraints that limit your accessibility to others?
- Do you feel in your heart that all people are brothers/sisters?
- Knowing this, can you allow this consciousness to enter into the way you behave with others?
- Can you sense when something honors this connection or exploits it?
- Can you share your sense of brotherhood/sisterhood openly, or do you feel you need to withhold your communal spirit because people will take advantage?
- How could you do more to foster the sense of brotherhood/sisterhood that you do have?

Unity

- How do you experience oneness? Is it a mental concept or do you feel this is true?
- How would you honor this sense of unity in your personal life?
- How would you foster unity in your work life?
- How would you teach unity to young children?
- Can you feel a sense of unity with the natural world? With animals? With strangers?
- How do you know we are united? At what level do you think this is so?
- Do you feel that the universe is one with all life?
- If you believe in unity, then are you aware of the delusion of separation?
- Can you see the falsehood behind any sense of separation?

Joy

- Where do you find joy in your life?
- What would you do to cultivate more joy?
- Can you define joy and what it feels like?
- Can you allow more joy to be part of your life?
- Do you find joy with people? In nature? In the animal kingdom?

WORKING THROUGH NEGATIVITY

- *Finding the love for oneself, in spite of whatever may have happened in the past, brings healing.*
- *Being able to forgive the past, including those who were hurtful or destructive, helps keep the heart open.*
- *Accept the present as the point of power where love can heal our wounds and restore a sense of wholeness.*
- *Learning to accept ourselves as we are, without pride or pretense, keeps the heart open and allows the good to come.*
- *Make a list of what makes your heart sing. Commit yourself to the process of reanimating joy by doing what you love, with people you love.*
- *Seeing the good in even the worst of situations and the most difficult of people helps keep the heart energy alive.*

The Throat Chakra, VISHUDDHA, is the first energetic center that differentiates humans from all other life forms. In the Kabbalah, man is referred to as "The Speaker." This attribute gives us the power to express ourselves on every level of experience. To honor this gift, we are asked to commit to expressing our truth and sing the song of individuality clearly and with integrity. To do so truly serves our spirits.

the THROAT
Chakra

VISHUDDHA
Purification

MOUTH OF GOD
The Throat Chakra is the gateway to higher spiritual realms and is called "the mouth of God" in esoteric teachings. This refers to a point on the back of the neck, near the *medulla oblongata* (the lowest part of the brain in vertebrates), where higher spiritual energy is channeled into the body. This occurs when the mind is free and the spirit open. It is where angels whisper in our ears and spiritual inspiration gives our lives meaning and cohesion.

EFFECTS OF ABUSE
The Throat Chakra is a vessel for subtle energy, and its integrity can be harmed through injury and emotional and physical

abuse. The Throat Chakra shuts down from grief and unexpressed feelings, such as anger and fear. It is compromised when we are dishonest or maligning, or gossip about others. The chakra is damaged by all forms of substance abuse that pass through the throat. Alcohol, smoking, both recreational and allopathic drugs, and overeating all pass through the narrow opening of the throat and profoundly disrupt the energy flowing from the lower chakras to the Brow and Crown Chakras.

Substance abuse diminishes the will and prevents us from fully harnessing our vitality. It mutes our feelings and confuses and disorients our mind. It cuts us off from expressing our highest truths when they are most needed.

INTEGRITY AND INDIVIDUALITY

We default on our integrity when we fail to honor our individuality. To maintain a strong and viable sense of selfhood, it is essential to express our truth as best we can, even at the risk of being different or standing apart from others. True adulthood is learning to mean what we say.

Gardenia

Qualities and Attributes

Location: The internal and external throat

Age of resonance: 35–42

Sensory experience: Hearing

Qualities: Will, communication, creativity, truthfulness, integrity

Life issues: To harness your will, to express your highest truth, to live creatively

Physical activities: Alexander technique, yoga, osteopathic alignment of the spine, craniosacral therapy, expressive theater and dance, qi gong, tai chi

Spiritual activities: Chanting, silent retreats, fasting, yoga, prayer, meditation, singing, keeping a journal, public speaking, bearing witness

Essential oils: Blue chamomile, gardenia, ylang ylang

Plant: Gardenia

Metal: Mercury

Element: The ethers, in which all things are contained

Musical note: G

Type of music: Opera

George Washington is a national archetype for honesty and integrity, both substantial qualities that depict a strong and resilient Throat Chakra.

Archetypes

POSITIVE:
The Communicator

This is a person who lives from personal integrity. Communicators tell the truth to the best of their ability. They are skilled in putting words to their feelings, and they are able to stand up for what they believe. They say no when they need to, and their word can be trusted.

NEGATIVE:
The Silent Child

This is a person who has suppressed expressiveness because of fear or shame. These people hide their feelings and are not connected to their higher truth. They say yes when they mean no.

THE THROAT CHAKRA AND THE PHYSICAL BODY

Associated Body Parts
Throat, mouth, teeth, jaw, ears

Physical Problems
Ailments associated with the Throat Chakra are sore throat, laryngitis, deafness, tooth decay, gum problems, T.M.J. (temporomandibular joint syndrome), and cervical problems of the neck.

Glandular Connection: Thyroid
The function of the thyroid gland is to regulate the basal metabolism, which has a direct effect on regulating the body's growth. It helps in developing teeth and enhancing muscular tone, and aids in mental development. It promotes the functional development of the sexual organs and the adrenal glands.

TRUTH AND HONOR

The Throat Chakra directly affects the quality of our communication. It is linked to our personal integrity and sense of honor. When we mean what we say and stand by our word, we influence the way in which people perceive us. They pay attention to what we say and recognize who we are.

As we deepen our commitment to expressing the truth, the Throat Chakra expands and becomes an invincible ally of the spirit, channeling energy for our physical vitality and spiritual development. We become stronger in ourselves and more resilient in our thinking when we express the truth. This provides us with sufficient energy to accomplish our purpose in life.

VITAL ENERGY

The reason we have more energy is that a strong Throat Chakra acts as a container for vital energy, keeping it intact so that energy does not drain away or become stagnant. When we live from our integrity and communicate honestly, an energetic seal forms around the Throat Chakra, and energy flows throughout the physical, mental, and emotional centers.

ASPECT OF THE SOLAR SYSTEM
Mercury

ASTROLOGICAL ASSOCIATIONS
Gemini and Virgo

**EARTHLY
LOCATION**
Italy

**ANGELIC
PRESENCE**
Archangel Gabriel, who
brings the word of God

**MYTHOLOGICAL
ANIMAL**
Sparrow hawk

RESULTS OF DYSFUNCTION

The energetic leaks of a dysfunctional Throat Chakra are experienced as fatigue, weakness, or dissipation. On a physical level, this manifests as an underfunctioning thyroid gland. Medication may be prescribed, but this does not change or alter the leak. Conventional medicine stimulates the thyroid and causes it to overproduce hormones. Energetically, it is essential to express a higher truth and connect to one's spirit for energy to be freely flowing in the system and for the ductless glands to secrete proper levels of hormones.

CONSERVING ENERGY

How we live and express our being directly influences the amount of energy we have. The Throat Chakra is also connected to willpower. Some people may find that they have to harness their will in order to accomplish simple daily tasks. The will is meant to be used for those spiritual trials that take us to higher levels, but that may be a challenge to our body. You can

The delicate fabric of the Throat Chakra is damaged by lying, malicious gossip, and substance abuse, all of which pass through the mouth and throat. These activities weaken the energetic quality of the chakra.

conserve the will for spiritual development if you are not using it for daily activity. To resonate joy and creativity in your job, relationships, or other aspects of your life, you must be spiritually truthful. You may be suppressing feelings that could indicate a need for change. Tuning into your higher truth helps conserve willpower for the challenges that really matter.

Harnessing the will fortifies the Throat Chakra. It helps keep you on the path of honest expression and helps develop character. In terms of a high feel-good factor, truth, energy, and emotions are all interconnected to the life of the body. Saying no to what and who may be harmful is essential to cultivating a strong will.

The Throat Chakra and the Emotional Body

The Throat Chakra gives expression to our emotions in word and sound. We purr when we are deeply happy, sigh when we are sad, grunt when we are angry, and close our throats down when we are afraid to say what is on our mind. It is the channel for communication and creativity. It is through the throat that we sing our joy, say our prayers for peace, or scream our pain away. Knowing that we have the right to communicate our feelings openly is essential for our life development.

THE HIGHER SELF
This chakra is directly linked to the higher self—that exalted aspect of being that offers guidance and protection. One's personal task is to tune in and listen to this guidance. If you are too busy listening to external chatter, or idly talking about other people, the guidance from the higher self gets lost in the cacophony. The internal auditory system is polluted with negativity from noise, lies, and hyper-exaggeration.

Our ability to communicate clearly determines the quality of our experiences. It also reflects the degree of intention we have to be understood and supported in life. These are essential qualities of the Throat Chakra.

The Throat Chakra and the Mental Body

The Throat Chakra is controlled by the mind. When we feel comfortable in expressing ourselves, the Throat Chakra is capable of expressing our truth eloquently and with grace. It is in the Throat Chakra that we tune our awareness into the higher mind, which whispers the truth to us through our inner ear. Developing a quiet mind allows us to hear the voice of spirit.

POSITIVE LISTENING

The Throat Chakra also governs the ears. We strengthen this chakra when we listen carefully to our inner voice. Our ability to listen silently opens the Throat Chakra and fortifies the link to the self. It has long been known that sound has the power to heal and can even strengthen the immune system. Hearing positive things about ourselves has a healing effect. Saying affirmations out loud, for instance, has a direct effect on the endorphin levels in our blood.

Hearing we are beautiful and everyone loves us lets our spirits shine. It tells us we are good and lovely. When we hear negativity about ourselves, we contract and separate from our core. If we are attached to external acknowledgment from others, we may believe what is said rather than know our own worth.

GUIDING FORCE

The power of the Throat Chakra is only as strong as our internal connection to the truth. If we are willing to be quiet and listen to our inner voice, it can act as a guiding force in our lives. We can expand the power of our internal guidance when we take the lid off our feelings and simply recognize them for what they are. This means allowing emotions to be experienced, though not necessarily acted out. Emotional suppression stops energy from flowing and it also keeps us from knowing our inner truth.

When the chakra is open and flowing, our inner beauty and external radiance flow freely. It takes someone who knows who they are and what they value to develop a strong Throat Chakra. It demands a willingness to overcome fear of speaking out and a desire to be emotionally mature and psychologically responsible.

CONNECTING TO THE TRUTH

Developing a wholesome relationship to the truth is the beginning of healing the Throat Chakra. Nearly all dysfunctional emotional experiences are suppressed in the throat. This happens when we fail to say what we feel, no matter how hurt or angry we are. We begin our empowerment when we tell the truth.

People can be completely changed by the experience of connecting to the truth. Energy, vitality, beauty, and a zest for life suddenly spring into their body and face. They know that speaking the truth connects them to that place within where they are truth itself.

THE SPIRITUAL DIMENSION

INTELLIGENCE:
Will and expression

SOUL LESSON:
Expressing divine will

The Throat Chakra's attitudes all nurture a belief in the sanctity of personal expression. This chakra becomes functional when we commit to expressing our truth to the best of our ability. Attitudes about suppressing "negative" feelings, being polite, and not rocking the boat block this chakra and weaken our life force. An essential attitude is that what we say matters, and this belief in self heals this chakra. If we grew up in a family that put down what we said, then speaking up for ourselves is important to us. Communicating from the depth of our integrity gives us credibility and constancy, and defines mature adults who can be trusted and mean what they say.

The scales of justice are a symbol of the weighing of evidence by a judge or jury. Justice relies on integrity and honesty, and these are only possible when we choose to live a conscious life, free from delusion, projection, and guilt.

How to Access the Throat Chakra

There are many ways in which to open up the throat. If feelings and true expression have been suppressed, one can benefit from therapy to help reanimate the feeling function. Singing or voice lessons are another way of strengthening the throat. Making a clear intention to express the truth paves the way for healing to happen.

Listening to the sound of your own voice can help you express yourself. Tape yourself reading your affirmations out loud and then play them back to yourself while you sleep.

TRUE TO YOUR FEELINGS

Most people are disconnected from their inner reality. It takes a conscious effort to be comfortable with feelings. If you feel angry, sad, anxious, or joyful, it serves your development to acknowledge these emotional states. It leads us to a better understanding of who we are. Being on the receiving end of insults or attacks, even those subtle put-downs made in jest, diminishes the spirit and weakens self-esteem. It is important to convey to those close to us that we are not willing to receive the brunt of their displeasure.

AFFIRMING YOUR WORTH

When we honor our personal truth and say how we feel, we grow internally. We detach from the need to please others and learn to nurture the spirit. Affirming our worth and honoring the choices we have personally made for happiness, health, and our welfare lets others know we are worthy of consideration. Speaking up, no matter how difficult it may seem, gives us confidence in who we are and conserves our vitality and integrity.

Speaking out is the gift of a free society that values freedom of speech. Speaking our truth is what differentiates us from all other life. Express the best of yourself with those who value who you are and respect your willingness to share yourself.

Negative Attitudes

The fear of expressing our truth blocks and limits our energy. If we feel that we have no right to speak out or that no one wants to listen to us, we dampen our life force and negate the precious gift of communication. Lying, substance abuse, and gossip are three things that damage the precious fiber of the Throat Chakra. All of them take us away from our natural goodness. When we lie, gossip, or trash our bodies with drugs, we lose credibility and respect.

Positive Attitudes

Honoring the truth and communicating it from a place of integrity is what makes us responsible adults. When we know we have something to say and it is worth expressing, we make a difference. We expand the Throat Chakra and open our energy field when we share our truth. Learning appropriate times and ways to express our truth is worth the effort because others can then respond to us.

Affirmations for the Throat Chakra

Repeat these affirmations once every morning and once every evening to strengthen and heal the Throat Chakra.

- *I live in my truth, I communicate my truth, I am the truth.*
- *Communicating is vital to my well-being.*
- *I love to share my experiences and tell my truth.*
- *I listen to the truth of others; I share my truth honestly.*
- *My willpower is aligned with my spiritual purpose in life.*
- *I develop will each time I meet a life challenge.*
- *I express my truth as creatively as possible.*
- *I communicate with those who open their hearts to me.*
- *I learn to listen to myself and trust my inner voice.*
- *I develop my integrity each time I tell the truth.*
- *My integrity is my word, and my word is my truth.*
- *My communication comes directly from my deep center.*
- *I express my love and goodness each time I speak.*
- *My spirit rests in peace and silence.*
- *I trust the whisper of angels' voices as I sit in silence.*
- *I share my feelings with ease and comfort.*
- *I communicate what is so for me, without projecting my truth onto others.*

Meditation for the Throat Chakra

Select a candle and some incense. Sit comfortably with your spine straight and take several deep breaths so that the muscles in your upper back and chest begin to relax. Drop your jaw and relax your tongue. Feel tension release from your scalp and feel your eyes pulling inward. Light the candle and burn the incense, and focus your attention on your mouth and throat.

SHAPE
Visualize a turquoise inverted pyramid suspended from your jaw

RADIATING ENERGY
Close your eyes and visualize a turquoise inverted pyramid suspended from your jaw. The apex of this pyramid is pointing down toward your heart. As you hold the image, expand the form and intensify the color. Feel the pyramid act as a seal that prevents energy from dissipating from your throat and becoming locked in your neck. Feel the tension in your neck, throat, and tongue loosen as you fill this area with turquoise light. Feel the energy radiating from your throat, expanding it and filling it.

FOUR QUALITIES
Begin to build the qualities of the Throat Chakra into the pyramid. The back wall contains the energy of your personal truth and the higher truth of God. It feeds energy into your ears, so that when you experience the truth, you know that you have been given guidance. The left side of the pyramid represents your willpower, which becomes strengthened each time you take a stand for yourself or complete a task. Resolve to complete, in the best way you can, what is unfinished in your relationships. It helps

Turquoise has been highly prized since ancient times and features strongly in Byzantine and Turkish architecture. It is the color that rules the Throat Chakra.

CRYSTALS

TURQUOISE

Highly prized by North American Indian and Asian cultures, turquoise is said to contain the spirit of the creator within it. Use it to increase creative energy in the Throat Chakra. It will heal any tendency to lose energy and help deepen a commitment to telling the truth.

BLUE AGATE

This stone helps anchor your spirit in your body. It helps preserve physical energy so that it is not dissipated in distracting conversations. It assists clear communication, truth telling, and strengthening the will.

AQUAMARINE

This is a beautiful stone that captures the beauty of the sea and the sky. It suggests balanced emotions and a deep commitment to sharing one's true feelings with someone you love for a lifetime of sharing.

you stay connected both to the spiritual realm and to the world.

The front wall represents the energy of communication. It feeds your vocal cords and larynx, helping you speak your truth and reach out to others. Choosing your words consciously supports you in making wholesome and rich connections with others. The right side contains creative energy that helps you express more of who you are. This can be used for art, writing, music, or anything that gives you joy. Creative outlets help you develop yourself.

Sit in silence now as you hold this energy in your throat center. Allow your ears to open to the truth and your willpower to strengthen. Feel the creative flow of energy stimulate your mind and your desire to share yourself with others.

SEAL THE CHAKRA

Seal this chakra with a cross of light within a circle of light. Let your ears remain open to hearing lovely things about yourself. Know that you hear the truth, you feel it, and you express it. Who you are is truth itself.

Questionnaire on the Throat Chakra

The questions for the Throat Chakra are centered on your levels of clear communication and conscious integrity. They can give you a guideline to understanding yourself better, so that you can achieve balance. For some, this may involve being more expressive; for others, it may revolve around the quality and truth in their communication.

THE COLOR OF THE THROAT CHAKRA: TURQUOISE

Turquoise suggests the beauty of the universal spirit, and represents all forms of creative expression, communication, truth, and willpower. The color is linked with the vast expanse of sea and sky, which engender feelings of beauty, depth, and freedom. It is a color used to soothe the soul. It is highly prized for decoration, clothing, and any place where beauty is expressed. Turquoise has a calming effect on the body and is said to be able to reduce blood pressure.

Communication

- How willingly do you share your truth with others? Do you say what you feel?
- Do you remain silent when you know you have something to contribute to others' lives?
- Are you open, clear, and honest in your communications?
- Do you express your feelings with ease?
- Do you judge others for expressing how they feel?
- Do you become frightened and closed when you have to express yourself?
- Do you know when it is appropriate to be silent?
- Do you always need external noise to keep you from your thoughts?

Integrity

- Do you know the importance of personal integrity?
- Do you do what you say you are going to do?
- Do you offer support to others and fulfill your commitment to be there for them?
- Are you truthful and honest with others? Can you be honest with yourself, even when opposed?
- How do you experience your integrity?
- Do you know when someone comes from their integrity?
- Can you tell when someone is lying and untruthful?
- How strongly do you value integrity?

Truth

- Do you honor your personal truth?
- Do you tune into your body, your feelings, and your spirit to know what your truth is?
- Do you value the truth of your heart as well as the truth of your mind?
- Do you know when others are being truthful?
- Do you feel a need to cover up your truth with certain people or in particular circumstances?
- How truthful are you when confronted by people who you dislike?
- Do you feel that telling the truth may be offensive to others?

Willpower

- How strong is your will?
- Do you use it for ordinary daily chores, or do you reserve it to meet extraordinary challenges?
- Do you feel you need to develop more willpower around exercise and food?
- Do you feel you have a strong will that lets you resolve problems that trouble you?
- Do you complete tasks that are set in front of you?
- Can you harness your will to develop discipline and wisdom?
- Do you feel you have will developed for challenging and difficult times?

Creativity

- Where do you channel your creative energy?
- What activities are the most creative for you?
- Do you make whatever task is in front of you creative and enjoyable?
- Can you see the connection between your creativity and your spirit?
- How would you be more creative in your life?
- What would you like to develop for yourself in terms of creative output?
- Do you enjoy being creative with your work? At home? In your wardrobe? With your garden?
- Does being creative make you feel good?

WORKING THROUGH NEGATIVITY

- *Make a commitment always to be as truthful as you can.*
- *Allow your creative spirit to manifest in every activity where you feel comfortable expressing yourself.*
- *Watch levels of substance abuse, such as smoking, overeating, and drinking. They weaken the will and destroy the Throat Chakra.*
- *Be careful what you say about others. Gossip can cause damage to others as well as to yourself.*
- *Build your credibility by coming from your integrity. People will respect you.*
- *Listen to your feelings. Know what is true for you.*
- *Listen to what is good, truthful, loving, and kind.*
- *Speak clearly and mean what you say. Your communication counts.*

The Brow Chakra, AjNa, is known as the control center because it focuses on cultivating a strong and independent mind. It contains the mental applications we need for creating happy and wholesome lives. It is usually fully activated in our mid-thirties when we have accrued some life experience to weigh against the ideas we ingested at an early age. If there has been psychological arrestment due to familial or cultural suppression, this chakra will struggle to work effectively against these constraints.

the **BROW**

Chakra

AjNa
To perceive, to know

HARMONIOUS THINKING

The Brow Chakra provides the energy for us to experience clear and concise thought, as well as the gifts of spiritual reflection and inner contemplation. It holds the roots for psychological maturity as well as ethical and philosophical principles.

When it is fully activated, this chakra stimulates both hemispheres of the brain. The right hemisphere controls synthetic thinking and creative activity. The left side controls rational, analytical thinking. Working together they create a harmonious vision of reality that incorporates logical thinking and imaginative experience.

Almond

AWAKENING THE MIND

The Brow Chakra provides the energy to expand our inner picture of how we see ourselves and the world. If we cultivate positive beliefs about self and others, our mental picture will be resilient and able to weather disruption.

This chakra is entirely about the power of mind to create our reality at the physical, mental, and emotional levels. It is in the realm of the mind that we transform our lives, harness our vitality, and implement our dreams. The Brow Chakra offers us energy to awaken our minds and question whether what we have been taught is true or false.

WISDOM AND KNOWLEDGE

To fully activate the Brow Chakra, it is necessary to examine self-limiting ideas that denigrate our worth. Its spiritual purpose is to offer us the possibility of wisdom, discernment, imagination, intuition, and knowledge. As we distill truth from life experience, we develop this chakra and strengthen our spirit.

Qualities and Attributes

Location: Between the eyebrows

Age of resonance: 35–42

Sensory experience: Mindful knowing/intuition

Qualities: Wisdom, discernment, imagination, intuition, knowledge

Life issues: To focus your intelligence, to know who and what are for your highest good and greatest joy, to distill wisdom from your life experiences, both good and difficult, to choose life, health, joy, and fulfillment in every aspect of your life

Physical activities: Yoga, tai chi, qi gong, Bates eye exercises

Spiritual activities: Thinking clearly about your life, reading or viewing uplifting and positive books or films, reflection, contemplation, meditation, and creative use of your imagination to visualize the life you say you want

Essential oils: Camphor, sweet pea, heliotrope

Plant: Almond blossom

Metal: Silver

Element: The cosmos

Musical note: A

Type of music: Classical, especially Mozart sonatas

Mozart

THE BROW CHAKRA AND THE PHYSICAL BODY

Associated Body Parts
Eyes, sinuses, base of skull, temporal lobes

Physical Problems
The problems associated with a dysfunctional Brow Chakra concern intelligence and stupidity, dull affectivity, and overwork. These problems can create conditions such as migraine, blindness and other eye problems (such as glaucoma and cataracts), brain tumors, and strokes.

Archetypes

POSITIVE:
The Wise Person

This is a person who has cultivated wisdom. Wise people offer the best of their experience to assist others. They encourage spiritual pursuits and physical adventures, and guide us in making wholesome choices for ourselves. Wise people live by universal principles and trust in a higher source to guide them through the peaks and valleys of life.

NEGATIVE:
The Intellectual

This is a person who draws only on information from rational, analytic thinking, without incorporating the emotional or spiritual aspects of life. Intellectuals seldom have a holistic assessment of a situation. They are limited in their scope, because they trust only conventional ideas. They are often judgmental and narrow in their outlook.

Glandular Connection: Pituitary
The pituitary gland is located between the eyebrows in a small cradle in the center of the sphenoid bone. When people are unable to think for themselves, or experience confusion, lack of mental clarity, or lack of imagination, the pituitary gland may be underfunctioning. It is called the master gland because it secretes a hormone that monitors the activities of the other glands in the body. Its hormones control skeletal growth and sexual development and maturation, as well as milk secretion in women. It has a strong influence on thyroidal and adrenal function. It controls blood pressure and is responsible for physical and psychological growth. When we are deeply attuned to our inner knowing, trusting our intuition, and using our creative imagination, this gland works well. When we come up against self-limiting beliefs about our worth, we impede the function of this gland.

SENSORY ENERGY

The Brow Chakra supplies energy to all the senses. It feeds energy into the eyes, ears, nose, and mouth and stimulates our sensory acuity. It provides energy to the brain to allow the mind to be active and positive. It opens portals to the higher spiritual realms that surround us and are accessible through developed sensitivity and open-mindedness. New arenas of possibility can be reached through a visionary mind able to think and intuit at the same time.

HEALING POWER

The power of healing is a function of our minds because it opens us to the good around us. It helps us acknowledge that we are whole, deserving of love and all that we say we want. It helps us expand the realm of new possibilities available to us and lets us see a horizon when we are tired or confused.

The Brow Chakra is especially responsive to both affirmations of our goodness and confirmation of our worth. When we affirm ourselves, we actually plant the seeds of goodness into the subconscious mind. They help us reprogram our vision to include greater possibilities for emotional happiness and physical well-being.

ASPECT OF THE SOLAR SYSTEM
The moon

ASTROLOGICAL ASSOCIATIONS
Sagittarius and Pisces

EARTHLY LOCATIONS
Peru and the Rocky Mountains

BELIEF SYSTEM

As we expand our minds, we learn that wholesome, optimal choices are within our grasp. It helps us to attune our spirit to universal intelligence, which is all loving, all seeing, and all knowing, no matter in what form we experience that intelligence. This universal intelligence responds affirmatively to what we believe about ourselves. If we believe we are worthy of love, goodness, prosperity, and health, it says yes. If we believe we are not worthy of what we say we want, or we feel we are ugly and no one loves us, this universal intelligence will, again, say yes. This force attests only to what we believe to be true. This means we need to choose carefully what we want to include in our worldview and examine our belief system to see what is true and has depth, constancy, and grace.

ANGELIC PRESENCE
The Shekhinah, better known as the feminine face of God

MYTHOLOGICAL ANIMAL
Hawk

FREEDOM OF CHOICE

Using wisdom and intelligence helps cultivate the higher mind to choose the good we want in our lives. The freedom to choose belongs to each individual. As the Brow Chakra develops and psychological maturity is reached, it becomes self-evident that we have the ability to change the way we look at our lives. We can expand the power of the mind to help us create healthier realities. The mind is dynamic and can open the doors to true healing.

POSITIVE THINKING

The Brow Chakra can control our physical bodies as well as our minds. It governs everything from our heart rate and blood pressure to our ability to withstand pain. Once the power of the mind is harnessed through meditation and yoga, it is capable of restoring health. Positive thinking increases endorphins in the blood stream. These substances control our "feel-good" factor and help us build reserves of energy we can tap into in times of stress or illness.

As the mind becomes healthier, so does the physical body. When we think positively, situations become positive. We learn to detach from holding onto destructive emotions that sabotage our health and choose to open to the love around us.

Walking on hot coals requires the mind to transform itself from one of limited possibilities to infinite potential. Many people find that they can heal their lives by releasing self-limiting ideas about what they can do.

The Brow Chakra and the Emotional Body

The Brow Chakra regulates our emotional responses. When a situation evokes our feelings, it is through the Brow Chakra that we decide how to respond. If we allow ourselves to feel, emotions can be experienced and disappear. If we suppress our emotions, they revert to the subconscious and block our energy.

The Brow Chakra lets us explore the realms of knowledge and develop inner knowing. It stimulates our imagination to envisage the life we say we want.

The Brow Chakra and the Mental Body

The Brow Chakra is where our mentality is formulated. It is the control center for the mind. Our intelligence can be used to create harmony or conflict. When we are at one with ourselves, we find we have few thoughts and our mind is still. When we are conflicted, we struggle with our mind, finding the best way to resolve our problems. The Brow Chakra operates holistically. It views life from a more inclusive perspective and points the way to more wholesome choices.

POWER OF THE MIND

We can use our mind to develop a healthy Brow Chakra by distilling wisdom from our past. This means we ask ourselves what we learned from a difficult or challenging situation or person. Another way of expanding the Brow Chakra is to turn the mind off and let it be still. This is one of the functions of meditation. This opens a portal to a higher spiritual realm, where we trust the source to guide us to freedom, love, and joy. Overusing the mind can distort reality.

When we trust the higher mind to work on our behalf, we find real and practical solutions for our lives. All the answers to our problems are within us. When we struggle to find answers to our problems outside ourselves, we deny ourselves the bounty of our own wisdom.

INTERNAL GUIDANCE

If we relinquish our spirit or give over our power to choose, we become objects in a game of prescribed formulas and quick fixes, which can control and limit us. These can range from our spiritual practice to impersonal interference in our lives. When we refuse to think for ourselves, or fail to weigh the pros and cons of any situation, we forfeit our right to make up our own minds.

As we develop the Brow Chakra, we are better able to access our internal guidance. Cultivating the wisdom of the higher mind creates reserves of energy that can keep us healthy and sane for our entire life. Being discerning helps us choose the right path and the right people. Applying knowledge can make our tasks in life easier. Using our intuition and imagination helps us create the best possible life we can.

REFLECTION AND TRANSFORMATION

Since this center controls most of what we do in our lives, including behavior, it is important that we develop realistic and grounded attitudes that support our being the best we can be. This is why we try to build a wholesome context for holding our life experiences, forgiving the past, and looking forward toward the light. Healing the mind means reflecting on oneself and transforming self-limiting ideas about who we are and what we deserve.

THE SPIRITUAL DIMENSION

INTELLIGENCE:
Control and wisdom

SOUL LESSON:
Detachment and intuition

The Brow Chakra matures with age and experience. It develops right thinking about who we are and helps us through the difficulties that challenge us. The ability to disengage from attacks, unwholesome situations, or people nurtures our inner clarity and strength. The ability to recognize the nature of people and situations frees us to use our life force appropriately. Healthy attitudes based on love and respect of self and others help us cultivate discernment. This teaches us to make optimal choices based on our highest good and greatest joy. Attitudes rich in flexibility, openness, and a deep love for one's self—and that same beautiful jewel in others—help us manage our lives with grace and wisdom.

The Eye of Horus is an ancient Egyptian sign of inner knowing. It reminds us of the higher power of the mind to access truth, intuitive awareness, and wisdom.

How to Access the Brow Chakra

The way in which we access the Brow Chakra is to examine how we think and feel about ourselves and our lives. If we are positive about who we are and how we feel about our experiences, then the Brow Chakra will be functioning well and we should have abundant energy available to us to do the things we love. If we have doubts about ourselves, it will become necessary to change the way we think in order to assist the chakra in doing its work. This is how we transform our energy.

The hawk is the symbol for clear and penetrating vision, and represents the capability of the Brow Chakra to cut through illusion to come to a higher truth.

HOLISTIC THINKING

Cultivating a positive and wholesome attitude about ourselves is the first key to healing the Brow Chakra. It suggests being able to recharge our energy when we are tired, re-thinking a solution we are struggling to solve, and being gentle on ourselves when we have had a difficult time. Accessing the Brow Chakra comes when we are willing to think and feel good things about ourselves. Otherwise, any negativity we harbor will shut the chakra down. Positive, holistic thinking is crucial to this chakra's function.

WISDOM AND SELF-LOVE

Learning to love and honor ourselves, during difficult times as well as when things are going well, requires us to cultivate wisdom and self-love. Taking the time to examine our attitudes is how we expand our inner reality and let go of harmful negative ideas about ourselves. This can be done alone, in therapy, or in spiritual practices that encourage self-inquiry.

Vanity is a negative attitude of the Brow Chakra. When we feel we need to be different in the eyes of others, we are saying that we are not lovable or worthy, and we fail to honor our true self.

Negative Attitudes

All negative ideas stem from the one belief that we are not enough. We are not lovable or worthy of having the life we say we want. When we identify with a lack of worth, we fail to honor our true self. Being forever cynical, anxious, and negative makes us ugly and old. Being inflated, separated from our true self, leads to egotism and narcissism. These attitudes develop when we feel we are not "enough" and need to be "more" in the eyes of others. Self-importance limits our truth as well as our vitality.

Positive Attitudes

The quintessential belief that we are worthy of receiving our good makes the mind healthy and whole. Accepting the best of ourselves helps us form clearly defined boundaries so that an attack cannot diminish us. Acknowledging our worth lets us know who and what are for our highest good. Loving ourselves lets us cultivate a sense of humor and makes our path through life more joyful. It also opens up our energy field.

Affirmations for the Brow Chakra

Repeat these affirmations once every morning and once every evening when you wish to access your Brow Chakra.

- *I think the very best of my self in all situations.*
- *I open myself to know my inner guidance and wisdom.*
- *I align my consciousness with the source of all life.*
- *I believe I am unlimited in my capacity for joy, healing, and happiness.*
- *I release and forgive the past.*
- *I open myself to new energy, people, and experiences.*
- *I trust that my highest good and greatest joy are unfolding.*
- *I am wise, intuitive, and aligned with my highest good.*
- *Every situation is an opportunity for growth and healing.*
- *I live in the light of my higher mind and allow it to illuminate my life.*
- *I seek wisdom and guidance in all situations.*
- *I open my imagination to see the best in people and things. I also see the best in myself.*
- *I am the source of truth and love in my life.*
- *As I tap into my inner wisdom, I know that all is well in my world.*

Meditation for the Brow Chakra

Begin by sitting in a place where you feel comfortable and safe to explore your inner reality. You can light a candle or burn incense if you choose. Relax by letting your eyes sink deep into your skull and letting your tongue relax in your throat. Release tension in your jaw by relaxing your chin, and let your shoulders drop as you take several deep breaths. When you feel receptive, begin the meditation for the Brow Chakra.

VISUALIZE A STAR

As you relax, visualize a large, indigo blue, five-pointed star. Locate this in your Brow Chakra, between your eyebrows. Expand the form and intensify the color. Go through each one of the five points and designate them as wisdom, discernment, imagination, intuition, and knowledge. Feel the flow of energy move through each of the points. It will expand the chakra and open your mind to developing these qualities within yourself. You can reflect on each of these qualities and visualize how they would manifest in your life. For instance, how would wisdom help you in a particular situation?

LIGHT OF CONSCIOUSNESS

Allow the light from this star to expand and fill your head. This is the light of consciousness that will bring you peace of mind and inner knowing. It is the light of truth that expresses your deepest longing for oneness, love, and beauty.

Let this light fill the dark recesses of your mind as you allow it to expand and fill you. See the beautiful, rich blue light fill your

SHAPE
Visualize an indigo blue, five-pointed star located between your eyebrows

eyes, ears, nose, and mouth and cover your entire face and skull. See that light filling your head and cooling off any agitated emotions or sense of frustration you may be feeling. Allow this light to run through every nerve ending in your brain, cool you off, and give you a deep sense of balance and well-being. Give yourself permission to sit quietly and explore this light of consciousness for several minutes. Are there images that come to your awareness, or words? If they repeat themselves, they may hold an important message for you. If any images appear in your mind's eye while you are meditating, allow them to be there; simply notice them and give them space.

SEAL THE CHAKRA

When you are ready to complete this meditation, visualize a cross of light within a circle of light sealing and protecting the Brow Chakra. This will seal in the energy that you have opened up. As you practice more often, you will find your mind is clear and receptive to ideas that can support you in your life development. You will feel restored and calm after doing this for a few minutes daily.

CRYSTALS

SAPPHIRE

This is a precious stone that contains the truest blues. It is a stone that stands for fidelity, clarity of thought, and a decisive mind. It can be used to sharpen the mind and lift the spirit. It is often chosen for wedding rings.

LAPIS LAZULI

This stone is known as the Philosopher's Stone, because it contains the colors of truth and integrity. It represents the wisdom principle of the higher mind. It can be used to create a spiritual context for holding one's life experiences.

TANZANITE

This stone is the most beautiful shade of blue, because it contains more violet than sapphire. It is also costly because it comes from only one mine, located in Tanzania. This stone can be used for healing, and stands for one's commitment to expressing truth, wisdom, and love.

The bindi is an ancient Hindi sign for the Third Eye, the seat of inner reflection and divine consciousness.

Questionnaire on the Brow Chakra

These questions are designed to help you see what areas of your Brow Chakra need attention and focus. They will touch deep and uncharted parts of your psyche. Allow the questions to bring up issues that need some attention. It is part of growth and healing.

THE COLOR OF THE BROW CHAKRA: INDIGO

This is the color of universal healing. It stands for detachment and represents a cool and clear level of consciousness. Indigo is the color used to unblock congested energy and cool down stressed-out nerves. It is the antidote to frustration and anger. Indigo brings our awareness to a higher plane by opening our consciousness to what is limitless and expansive. Indigo can also seem cold and lacking in human warmth if not counterbalanced with yellow or orange. It can leave us too detached and feeling emotionally disconnected. It is cool, antiseptic, and unearthly because it is the color of spirit, the higher mind, and clarity.

Wisdom

- Do you respect the wisdom that comes from the life experience of your friends and elders?
- What is your personal wisdom about your health, happiness, relationships, finances, and healing?
- Do you feel safe sharing your wisdom with others? Do you listen for the wisdom people share with you?
- Can you look at the challenging experiences in your life and distill wisdom from them?
- In your wisdom, can you forgive the past and extract the learning that was there for you?
- Can you find the wisdom to love and accept yourself after a difficult day or experience?

Discernment

- How do you discern what and who are for your greatest good?
- Do you let others drain you because you cannot discern a healthy boundary or want to please others?
- Do you trust your ability to discern good from bad, mediocre from wholesome?
- Are you able to say no to what is not good for you? Can you discern those who are on your side and those who are exploitative and manipulative?
- Can you look at the situations and people in your life and draw a line to protect your spirit from being hurt by those who do not cherish you?
- Can you discern what is really valuable and beautiful about yourself and honor that within you?

Knowledge

- Do you value knowledge that can make your life more fulfilling and meaningful?
- Are you willing to take time to accrue knowledge about the things you love and enjoy in life?
- Would a refined and qualitative form of knowledge make your life better in some essential ways?
- What areas of your life would you like to develop by gaining more knowledge?
- Do you respect your ability to learn and stimulate your mind with good books, films, and experiences?
- Knowledge is a survival tool for your soul. Are you able to know what is important to know and what is a waste of your time and energy?

Imagination

- Do you allow yourself to daydream about what your life would be like, if only...?
- Can you visualize what your life will be like in one year? Five years? Ten years?
- Imagine what you would be like if you had your dreams realized. What would be different?
- What are the things you would like to see improved?
- Can you imagine being loved and cherished in a way that respects who you are?
- Can you imagine being financially stable with enough money to do what you want?
- Can you imagine having a level of health and vitality where you have the energy to do what you love?

Intuition

- How do you know what you know? Can you use your inner knowing to intuit what is best for you?
- Do you ever allow your intuitive powers to show you a future, or the true nature of a person or a situation?
- Can you trust what your intuition tells you about something or someone?
- Are you willing to tap into the storehouse of knowing available to you?
- How do you use your intuition at present? Do you ever know that something is the way it is, regardless of what others try to tell you?

WORKING THROUGH NEGATIVITY

- *Allow your mind to relax. Overuse leads to worry and obsessions.*
- *Question anything that negates your innate worth, sense of freedom, or beauty.*
- *Look for the good in each person and each situation.*
- *Note any abusive patterns in your life and tell yourself, "Never again."*
- *Stop comparing yourself with others. Find what is unique about you.*
- *Meet like-minded people on courses and in workshops. Doing so can assuage fear and loneliness.*
- *Read and see inspirational books and films.*
- *Make a choice to be as loving and positive as you can be.*
- *Be aware when you are tired and weary. Do something positive for yourself.*

The Crown Chakra, SAHASRARA, reaches the heights of spirituality. It connects us with our indelible and permanent divinity, and is the source of healing energy in the human energy system. The chakras act as a ladder to love, spirituality, and healing, from the base energy of the Root Chakra, which anchors us in life, to the more refined spiritual energy of the Crown Chakra. Like all the other energy centers, the Crown Chakra exists as a vestigial core of potential until it is activated.

the CROWN
Chakra

SAHASRARA
Thousandfold

MATURITY AND INSIGHT

The Crown Chakra opens when we have attained psychological maturity and spiritual development. The opening of the Crown Chakra coincides with a time in our lives when we may have to face several difficult personal choices and external life challenges. These ultimately bring us spiritual insights and a greater sense of what we are capable of, and what our higher purpose might be. For many, such realizations are often seen as a form of "midlife" crisis—enlightenment often leads us to reject what we have been, in pursuit of what we could become.

SPIRITUAL PATH

The Crown Chakra is the center where we experience and know a higher God as an active presence in our lives and where we can choose to follow his ways. It is the driving force for mystics and healers immersed in cosmic consciousness, and for all those who actively seek and cultivate their spiritual path.

DIVINE BALANCE

In order for the Crown Chakra to open, it is no longer necessary for us to renounce the world and its material temptations entirely. Our goal must be to see the spirit in all life and to understand that we are here on earth to be happy and fulfill our soul's longings for love, peace, and happiness. When the Crown Chakra does open, we need rest, tranquility, and peace in order to contemplate the wonders and mysteries of the divine. By balancing worldly activity with spiritual pursuits, we can remain grounded in life, often bringing healing and transformation in subtle ways to our immediate world.

Violet

Qualities and Attributes

Location: Top of the skull

Age of resonance: 42–49

Sensory experience: Bliss

Qualities: Grace, beauty, serenity, oneness with all that is

Life issues: Selfless realization of your indelible connection with the greater whole of life, creation of a vital and resilient spiritual context for holding your life experiences

Physical activities: None—stillness

Spiritual activities: Prayer, meditation, reflection

Essential oils: Violet, lavender, lotus, elemi

Plant: Lotus flower

Metal: Platinum

Element: The cosmos

Musical note: B

Type of music: Indian ragas

Lotus

The bishop's miter represents the divine presence located in the Crown Chakra. The headdress of a Native American chief marks a particular state of enlightenment associated with the Crown Chakra.

Archetypes

POSITIVE:
The Guru

Gurus are people who realize who they are. They know that the divine force flows through them, and they are identified with that as the substratum of their being, rather than the temporal parts of their life. They let life move through them and take them ever deeper into consciousness itself.

NEGATIVE:
The Egotist

Egotists are people who think their efforts alone carry them through life. They believe that they are separate from a greater whole of existence, and that their striving and effort controls the outcome of their life.

THE CROWN CHAKRA AND THE PHYSICAL BODY

Associated Body Parts
Upper skull, cerebral cortex, skin

Physical Problems
When the Crown Chakra is dysfunctional, there are problems with learning, perception, and spiritual understanding. The physical problems that can occur are epilepsy, color blindness, alcoholism, nervous disorders, neurosis, and insomnia.

Glandular Connection: Pineal
This gland is located at the top of the head. It resembles the rod and cone of the eye and seems to be light-sensitive. It controls sleep patterns, menstrual cycles, and deep rhythmic cycles of the body. It is associated with higher consciousness and is the realm of the divine. We activate this gland when we do meditation, yoga, and self-realization inquiry. It is felt to be our link with cosmic energy, which enters the physical body through this chakra and stimulates this gland. It is known that in certain Eastern esoteric practices, focus on the pineal gland opens the higher mind to illumination and a sense of oneness with all things.

POSITIVE OUTLOOK

This center eases physical and emotional
pain and releases endorphins that create
happy and blissful experiences for us. This
hormonal release can be activated through
meditation, yoga exercises, and developing
a sense of love for beauty and for life.
When the Crown Chakra opens, it brings
attitudinal changes and a more positive
outlook toward life. It helps a person
develop a spiritual context for challenges
and difficulties. It induces both gratitude
and acceptance. The rule of the ego, which
is the part of us that divides, limits, and
judges, no longer has dominion over the
mind. Instead, there is compassion and a
sense of oneness with life and an acceptance
of one's self.

HIGHER PURPOSE

Healing happens when the mind is loving,
inclusive, embracing, and allowing. As the
Crown Chakra opens, we gain the awareness
that, although reality may appear to be
diverse in nature, it is ultimately undivided,
whole, and benign. Our higher mind learns
to accept that we are loved, guided, and
protected by a source higher and more
powerful than ourselves, and that we are
each here for a purpose.

ASPECT OF THE SOLAR SYSTEM
The universe

✦

ASTROLOGICAL ASSOCIATION
Aquarius

**EARTHLY
LOCATION**

India

**ANGELIC
PRESENCE**

The Christ Light

**MYTHOLOGICAL
ANIMAL**

Eagle

SPIRITUAL STRENGTH

Once we start living from and within the Crown Chakra, we start to be thankful for our lives exactly as they are. In having formed a spiritual context in which we can retain our life experiences, we accept the trials and hardships that have shaped our spirit. By realizing that our lives could not be any other than what they are, we are able to relish being exactly as we are now. We know—or are awakened to the awareness—that who we are is divine in nature and nothing can stop our spirit. This mental and emotional transformation supports our audacity for seeking a better life and gives us the inner strength to pursue our rightful path.

DIVINE GUIDANCE

Whichever way we experience the divine, we accept that our lives are not in our hands alone. By surrendering our fears and burdens to a higher power, we are able to cope better and more calmly with any pain, loss, or separation we may encounter. When we begin the process of conversion—of accepting that our lives are divinely guided— we lighten up, become healthier and more resilient, and open up to new realms of possibilities for living as we would like. The more we attune our awareness to the ultimate truth of a higher power, the freer we become to live in joy, harmony, and serenity. Honoring the spirit permits us to experience gratitude for who we are and how life unfolds. We learn that we are never alone, and that we are guided, loved, and protected at all times.

THE SPIRITUAL DIMENSION

INTELLIGENCE:
Spiritual understanding

SOUL LESSON:
To be at one with the source

A healthy Crown Chakra opens us to a spiritual understanding of the oneness of life. It is predicated on the belief that there is no separation at any level in an expanded reality that acknowledges the source of life. We learn that we are always guided and protected. A higher power moves our lives in a caring and loving way. When we connect this understanding with our life experiences, we are able to salvage our spirit through challenging times by seeing how each event opens us to a greater love and connection with spirit.

Monasteries, cloisters, and ashrams provide the peace and simplicity for reflection on the inner self. They act as sanctuaries for the spiritual to retreat from worldly temptation, and allow attention and concentration on all things divine.

The Crown Chakra and the Emotional Body

The Crown Chakra has but one emotion and that is bliss. This state is described as a joyful sense of the divine. Once it is experienced, it tends to negate all other emotions. A state of bliss is felt when there is no longer identification with the lower centers. This state of bliss is often called transcendence.

The Crown Chakra and the Mental Body

The Crown Chakra opens the realm of higher thinking to us. Here we see the entire picture and move beyond the petty details of life. The Crown Chakra is global, even universal, in its approach to situations or people. It has a spiritual dimension that teaches us to consider the origin of conflict, and to see with our heart as well as our head. It is able to put things into perspective.

How to Access the Crown Chakra

Many practices attempt to maximize the spiritual and psychic powers associated with the Crown Chakra. Such practices include purposeful solitude, deep reflection, silence, prolonged fasting, all-night prayer vigils, and visionary quests alone in nature. Such techniques have been used since ancient times to fortify an internal spiritual connection to the divine.

GROUNDING TECHNIQUES

Staying grounded in your body helps to stabilize the Crown Chakra. Eating wholesome foods, drinking unchlorinated water, and getting plenty of rest and exercise are ways of staying stable as this chakra unfolds. Daily practice of prayer, meditation, reflection, yoga, or tai chi helps ground the spirit. Never try to force open this chakra—like the lotus, it will flower naturally, when you are ready to accept it.

STATE OF ENLIGHTENMENT

The power of the Crown Chakra reaches its highest level of attainment in a state of awareness known as Samadhi. This refers to union with the Godhead where the ego dissolves into the universal force, becoming one with it. Samadhi, or Enlightenment, is a state of grace where a person experiences the oneness of all life. It is the most elevated state of awareness known to human consciousness because a person is linked directly with the source and becomes one with all that is. When people have achieved Enlightenment they know their spirit is eternal, unblemished, and always at peace.

Affirmations for the Crown Chakra

Repeat these affirmations once every morning and evening as you enter a period of Crown Chakra enlightenment.

- *God is in me, above me, below me, and around me at all times.*
- *I seek the highest truth and the most healing ways to live my life.*
- *I honor and protect my divine spirit.*
- *I know that all is good despite appearances to the contrary. I look within where I am safe and loved.*
- *My spirit is eternal. It loves harmony, peace, and joy.*
- *I trust that my highest good and greatest joy are unfolding now.*
- *I accept who I am and honor the spirit within me.*
- *I live in joy and gratitude for the goodness that fills my life.*
- *I appreciate the beauty of the earth and will honor and protect it as well as I can.*
- *I know my higher purpose is being fulfilled now.*
- *I trust God to show me the next step in my process.*
- *Goodness and joy are mine in all situations.*
- *I am thankful for the awareness and insight I have into the profound mystery of life.*
- *Thank you for my life, for who I am and for what you have allowed me to become.*

The mandala is a representation of the self. It is often seen in churches and temples to describe the compellingly beautiful nature of our inner being. It is an aid to meditation and can be used as a tool for entering the inner realms of peace and being.

Negative Attitudes

The most egotistical belief is that we are doing it all alone. This belief fortifies the ego and gives it license to exploit and manipulate. We thus fail to recognize a higher power than our limited self. This attitude fosters arrogance, false pride, and an over-inflated ego that lives under the pretense that it is invincible and unconquerable. It separates a person from contact with humanity, and keeps the heart closed to love and healing.

Positive Attitudes

Healthy Crown Chakra attitudes embrace a sense of gratitude for one's life and humility for goodness. When we realize God loves, protects, and guides us, we anchor our consciousness in a reality based on faith rather than anxiety. Our everyday life becomes infused with spirit and grace, and we let go of the petty irritations that cause us distress. Spiritual awareness deepens our life, giving it meaning and a sense of higher purpose.

Meditation for the Crown Chakra

Visualize a violet skullcap sitting on top of your head. Expand the form of the cap and intensify the color. Feel the healing quality of violet surround you like a protective cloak against pain, discomfort, and suffering. As you begin to feel the energy of this color, take a deep breath to inhale its healing properties.

SHAPE
Visualize a violet skullcap sitting on top of your head

JOYFUL REFLECTION

Begin to reflect on your breath. As you breathe in, call in the joy that you deserve. As you breathe out, exhale what is old, tired, and stale in your life. Keep this up for a few minutes. Reflect on all the joyful things around you: the stars at night, the moon in her beauty, the sun in its splendor. Know how healing the rain can be as it turns the leaves green. Feel the air around you, see the faces of people whom you love and enjoy. Keep your breathing focused on letting this joy into your life and releasing any negative influences.

As you open your higher center, take a moment to give thanks for your life. Even if your life does not appear to be the way you would like it to be, acknowledge that you are grateful to be here experiencing the wonders of your higher mind.

SWEET SURRENDER

Take a few deep breaths and allow your consciousness to turn more inward. Release the events and experiences of the day, or the emotions that you have been attached to for one reason or another. This realm of pure consciousness is one of being, ease, stillness, and sweet surrender to the moment. You need do nothing. In this space all is light, love, joy, and the tender awareness that you are one with all life. In being your self, you are free, intelligent, beautiful, and the source of power in your life. When you access the self, there is nothing to do but be. Allow the light of love, healing, and peace to embrace you, and pull your awareness deeper within.

Feel your body awareness begin to fade away. Feel your thoughts disappear. Be aware of your breath, your heartbeat, the stillness of your mind. You are the witness of your own life, unfolding as each moment melts into the eternal now. Keep your breath focused on allowing joy into your life.

SEAL THE CHAKRA

When you feel saturated by the positive energy that is filling your field, seal your Crown Chakra with a mental cross of light surrounded by a circle of light. This symbol will seal and protect the Crown Chakra until you are ready to do this meditation again. As you come out of the meditation, allow a sense of peace and detachment to carry you through the day. Find beauty wherever you can. Try to look for it when situations are difficult. You will find it. Remember all joy and goodness are yours now and forever.

Being spiritual requires an openness to knowing who you truly are. Meditation can help you connect with your inner self.

CRYSTALS

AMETHYST

This stone is associated with the Crown Chakra because it brings spiritual clarity and love of the higher mind. It can be used in healing to diffuse pain.

ALEXANDRITE

This is a rare stone that is highly charged with a refined electric energy. It stimulates psychic gifts, such as clairvoyance and clairaudience, and opens up the higher centers of awareness.

Questionnaire on the Crown Chakra

The qualities of the Crown Chakra are spirituality, beauty, and bliss. Look at these questions and see how you can develop or strengthen your connections to this most powerful energy source. As you read the questions, ask yourself if you need anything, other than your own awareness of self, to be spiritual. Being spiritual requires an openness to knowing who you truly are. There is a joy and lightness that come when you develop a strong and resilient connection to the self.

THE COLOR OF THE CROWN CHAKRA: VIOLET

This is the color of cosmic awareness. It is known as an antiseptic color that can soothe pain and relieve tension in the body. Violet acts as a shield against negativity and is a protective color for those seeking spirituality. It is felt to help dissolve the ego. For people who have a fragile ego this color can cause confusion. It is always best to balance it with its complementary color of yellow, which stands for a strong sense of self-identity.

Spirituality

- Do you have a spiritual context for holding the difficult and challenging experiences of your life?
- Can you open yourself to the love, guidance, and protection of a force greater than your limited self?
- Do you feel connected to the ultimate reality?
- What are your highest spiritual truths about yourself, life, death, and change?
- Are you capable of changing any negative ideas that limit your sense of oneness with all life?
- Do you empower religion, the Church, a guru, clairvoyants, or healers to give you the answer to life?
- Do you feel that you have to do things to be loved or accepted by the source?
- What do you empower to connect you with that which is already a part of you?
- By doing rituals, chanting, meditating, fasting, or prostrating yourself, do you know the source any better?
- Do you feel you can be loved, healed, and cherished by simply being yourself?

Beauty

- Do you find beauty stimulates your appreciation for life?
- Do you allow your own beauty to shine?
- Can you see the beauty in others?
- When you are around dysfunctional or ill people, can you see their inner beauty?
- How beautiful do you make your surroundings?
- What is the most beautiful thing in nature you have witnessed?
- Can you see that beauty is part of the wonder of life?

Bliss

- Do you need anything to happen to feel your bliss?
- Do you need to solve the problems of your life to feel your bliss?
- Do you need others to change in order to feel your bliss?
- Do you need to receive anything in order to feel your bliss?
- Can you create the time you need to be still and feel your bliss?
- Can you let go of all external conditions being right for you to feel your bliss?
- What do you need to do to allow your bliss to be a part of your experience?
- Are you willing to give up your attachment to the negative things in your life to be in bliss?

WORKING THROUGH NEGATIVITY

- *Open your awareness to a higher power than your limited everyday self. This higher self can guide your way, and offer you love and protection. Take the time to find this within yourself.*
- *Look inside yourself to discover who you are. Release limited ideas of self so they fall away easily.*
- *Read scripture and spiritually uplifting books.*
- *Avoid becoming entangled in situations or with people who reject peace.*
- *Explore your true beliefs about life. Do not accept what has been handed to you without knowing whether it is right for you.*
- *Direct your awareness inward for a moment every day to connect with the part of you that is eternal and indelible. It will guide you through your life if you allow it to.*

Dancing connects us with the higher realms of the divine. It is said that Lord Shiva danced the world into creation. Each time we experience joy in our own natural state of being, we strengthen the link to God.

CHAKRA HEALING

Learning how to heal your chakras gives you the power to bring balance and joy into your life. Once you take responsibility for how your energy is, you can use light, thought, and energy medicine to restore health at all levels.

There are many healing modalities you can use to bring healing and balance to the chakras. Consider which methods you wish to explore more thoroughly. The one you feel the most attracted to may bring the best results. Read through the different methods carefully and consider which treatment will benefit you; then wisely allow it to work its course.

HEALING METHODS

Dream Journal

When we are in the process of healing, it is important to be aware of dreams and the metaphors they represent for the situations in our lives. Dreams carry psychological content that can unlock our energy system. Keeping a journal during your healing can help you to remember your dreams and reveal important insights.

BEING WELL IN YOURSELF

In the beginning, there may be no visible effects that allow you to say a condition is improving or that you are better. In the realm of subtle energy, you will have only your experience to attest to the degree of healing that has occurred. You may feel a greater sense of well-being and joy. Your outlook toward others, toward yourself, and toward the situations you are in may shift so that your perception is more positive and your spirit is uplifted. This is known as being well in yourself. This is how subtle chakra healing works. It asks that you be aware of yourself and notice how you are feeling. Cure happens from the inside out and from the top down.

THE LAW OF CURE

You may notice inner changes before you see external change. When symptoms shift from the top of the body and move down toward the feet, they are following the ancient Law of Cure that governs how physical symptoms leave the body.

DETOXIFICATION PROCESS

While you are healing, there may be times you feel exhausted. This is a time to allow the body to release old, stagnant energy. You may need several early nights and even naps to help the body regenerate itself. You may feel emotional and in need of a good cry or to express anger or rage. Whatever has been suppressed will find its way to the surface. Allowing the truth of your emotions to be apparent will help you heal.

In order for the body to redress old wounds and restore balance, it may need to release toxins. This can be done through diarrhea, fever, a cold and sore throat, or flulike symptoms. Allow the body to let go of whatever it needs to. On an emotional level, you may find that you feel irritated, low-spirited, or angry for a few days. The more symptoms appear on the surface of the body, the greater the detoxification process.

HOLISTIC HEALING

In the realm of energetic healing, you may become aware of moods and a change in cycles such as sleep, menstruation, and appetite. Be patient and give your body time to right itself. If, however, you become aware that something is not right after a treatment, consult your physician or healer immediately. It is important to be able to depend on your healer when something is changing. Being able to talk to your healer is a part of good holistic healing practices.

This geyser perfectly describes how energetic healing breaks open what is congested, imploded, and suppressed. It is one of the great rediscoveries of our time that energy can be used to bring healing and balance to our fragmented lives.

CONSISTENT THERAPY

Different healing modalities vary in their intensity. Some may need to be repeated over a period of time; with others, you will notice that you feel more positive immediately. Being consistent with a therapy helps it to work on your behalf. Changing a modality too soon and not allowing its action to work on your energy system diminishes its effects.

Color Healing

Color healing has been the traditional way of working on the chakras for thousands of years. It was employed in ancient Egypt and is still used in India today. Because each chakra is associated with a color, sound, and gemstone, these are often combined to help reestablish balance in the human energy system. The principle idea is to match the color with the chakra in need of healing.

Color healing was used in ancient Egypt to bring balance and healing. The Egyptians loved the sun and worshipped its light. They knew that light and color could restore peace of mind, balance the emotions, and release physical pain. We are once again finding new ways, such as pinhole glasses, to use color to treat some of our most serious imbalances.

USING COLOR HEALING

There are different ways of bringing the color into the energy field. Some healers use colored silk scarves. They may wrap the body in them or suggest wearing the color on the part of the body that corresponds with the dysfunctional chakra. It is possible to transform the chakra by wearing the color that is needed.

There are healers who project the color from their Brow Chakra into the auric field of their patient. This is done only with imagination and intention. It is very effective for balancing the chakra. As a supplement, holding or placing the appropriate gemstone on the chakra helps release negative energy.

Color can be employed with the use of pinhole glasses made in the color of the chakra. The eyes absorb the color and send it to the appropriate chakra. This method requires a commitment of 10–15 minutes a day for wearing the glasses, but it is powerfully effective.

INDIAN METHODS

In India, there are two methods of using color to heal the subtle energy field. One is to take a glass pitcher of spring water and cover it with colored silk for the chakra that needs healing. The pitcher of water is put out into the sun so that the color can be absorbed into the water. Then the patient drinks the water at the corresponding hour of the chakra every day. If the Sacral Chakra needed healing, for example, one would cover the pitcher with orange silk and drink the water between 10 and 11 A.M., the hour of this chakra's optimal energy.

Another method is to place a jar of honey in the sun for a few hours with a silk cloth of the color desired laid over the honey. The color is absorbed into the honey, where it is preserved. A spoonful of this honey each day will help heal the chakra.

COMBINING TECHNIQUES

Today, modern color healers use a variety of techniques. One method suggests wearing the gemstone, eating the foods, drinking solarized water, and sitting or standing under floodlights with colored filters. These are effective treatments that are noninvasive and gentle. They are excellent for debilitated people, and can help restore their vitality and peace of mind without drugs. If, however, conditions prevail, it is important to consult a physician.

An Indian method of color healing involves covering a pot of honey with a colored scarf, so that the honey absorbs the color.

Homeopathy

Homeopathy uses the principle that like cures like. It was developed by Samuel Hahnemann in the early 19th century in Germany. Hahnemann discovered that a substance that could create symptoms could cure those symptoms using small dilutions of that substance.

Acupuncture

Acupuncture—an ancient Chinese procedure—does not relate to chakras as much as to vessels of energy. It works on a system of "meridian points" that correspond to various organ functions in the body. The meridians are linked to chakras by virtue of the fact that certain organs correspond to chakras. Today, in Germany, a form of "colorpuncture" has been developed that uses needles dipped in solarized, colored water and placed on meridian points. This affects the chakras directly and brings balance and healing.

USING HOMEOPATHY

Today, homeopathy has an extensive materia medica that is based on substances, both toxic and nontoxic, that come from nature. These substances are highly diluted to allow any toxicity to be removed. All the patient receives is the quintessential energetic pattern of the substance, and this is used to stimulate the body's natural healing vitality.

Color has recently been included in the homeopathy materia medica. Remedies have been made from light-saturated water using colored gels and mirrors, then diluted. Other ways in which color is used in homeopathy is from the use of remedies that fit into the color spectrum. All substances fit into the color spectrum; therefore, remedies made from these substances fall into color categories. For instance, iron is red and it carries the same vibration as that color. Sulfur is yellow and manganese is violet; they each carry a color vibration that works on the chakras that correspond to that color.

Today, there are remedies made from precious gemstones that also carry the vibration of a chakra and a color. Emerald, ruby, aquamarine, and topaz, for instance, are now made in dilution to treat conditions that arise in the corresponding chakras.

Flower Essences

The wonderful Bach flower remedies were developed by Dr. Edward Bach, a British homeopath, in the 1930s. Bach hoped to cultivate remedies that would work specifically on the Emotional body. He felt that flowers offered the gentleness required to heal fraught and discordant emotions.

USING THE ESSENCES

Bach's remedies are made in a different way than a homeopathic remedy. They are not diluted, but made from soaking the flower in spring water and placing that liquid in the sun for several hours. This is called a "mother tincture" and is used specifically to heal emotional dysfunction.

Bach's work opened a pathway for other flower essences to be used for healing. Today, the Australian Flower Essences, remedies from the Flower Essence Society of California, and several other regional and national essences offer healing for distraught emotions and physical problems. They work through the chakras by color and emotional affinity.

Flower essences carry the healing vibrations of plants and flowers to stabilize the emotions and restore balance. They are gentle, safe, and highly effective for treating imbalances in the Emotional body.

Hands-on Healing

There are different forms of hands-on healing in which a healer will balance the chakras. In general, hands-on healing is done through infusing the subtle body with charged magnetic energy from the practitioner's own field. This helps to release blocked energy that has congested and caused energy stagnation.

There are many different hands-on methods developed by healers. All address the subtle energy field to restore peace, movement, and vitality.

DIAGNOSING THE PROBLEM

A healer is able to read levels of clarity and vitality in the chakra through observing the aura and asking patients to talk about the specific problems in their life. If a person is having problems with love, the diagnosis is clear: the Heart Chakra is blocked. If the problem is the inability to reason or find a path of direction, the Brow Chakra would be worked on. If the problem is physical vitality, the Sacral Chakra would need attention. Some healers see colors, others hear guidance, still others use affirmations to ease distress.

Understanding the chakras and their emotional components helps you to diagnose where there is imbalance and where healing is needed. Some healers begin by asking the patient to lie on a table and begin to relax. They may massage their hands, feet, and head to get the patient to relax and release fears and tension. Crystals may be used to anchor the spirit in the body, making it easier for the patient to remain aware of and sensitive to emotions, thoughts, or pictures that arise during the treatment.

BALANCING THE CHAKRAS

After the diagnosis, the patient turns onto the stomach and the healer's hands can be placed on one chakra at a time to balance the energy system. The healer can move her hand back and forth in clockwise circles over the chakra or in a figure-eight motion. This can be done over clothing and even through a blanket.

It can be soothing and healing to play quiet and gentle music to calm the nerves and still the mind as the healer works on the chakras. A gentle chakra massage releases accumulated energy and opens the field for positive thoughts to be received.

This massage can be done over each one of the chakras. As the healer moves up the body, less time is spent on each chakra. The closer you get to the sensorium, which is part of the nervous system, the less time it takes to shift the energy in the chakras.

SEALING THE CHAKRAS

After the massage, the chakras are sealed in order to keep their energy field clear and resilient. The chakra is sealed by taking a small candle and making a cross of light within a circle of light, moving clockwise around the chakra. This can be done in the front and the back of the body to seal in the delicate and volatile energy of each chakra.

After each chakra has been circled, the entire auric field is sealed as the practitioner moves clockwise around the body three times. This seals in the good, healing energy and protects the chakras.

Using a Pendulum

Some healers use a pendulum to read the energy of a chakra. This helps determine the degree of congestion and the regularity of movement in the chakra. The healer holds the pendulum over the chakra and watches it gyrate. Even movement in a clockwise direction indicates that the chakra energy is flowing in the proper direction. Movement of the pendulum in a counterclockwise direction indicates that the chakra is blocked and in a negative spin. When this occurs, it is suggested that using affirmations can turn the spin of the pendulum back in a positive direction. Having the patient repeat healing sentences, such as "I love myself," "I am whole and complete," and "I am a child of God and embraced by his love," can bring balance and healing quickly.

Crystal Healing

Crystals can be worn or placed on the body to energize or balance the various chakras. They can be found in most crystal shops and must be cleansed in cold water and salt and energized by being placed in the sun or in moonlight. Sun activates the male principle and gives strength, fortitude, and resilience. The moon activates the feminine principle of receptivity, harmony, and openness.

CHAKRA CRYSTALS

Root Chakra: *ruby, garnet, bloodstone, hematite, pyrite*

Sacral Chakra: *carnelian, tiger's eye, agate, quartz, calcite, rutilated quartz*

Solar Plexus Chakra: *topaz, citrine, yellow diamond, opal*

Heart Chakra: *emerald, peridot, jade, rose quartz, ruby*

Throat Chakra: *chalcedony, aquamarine, turquoise, jade, chrysocolla*

Brow Chakra: *sapphire, iolite, tanzanite, lapis lazuli, soapstone*

Crown Chakra: *amethyst, fire opal, alexandrite, labradorite*

USING CRYSTALS

When healing a specific chakra, the crystals should be worn around the neck, or they are placed over the body, on the chakras, for a quarter of an hour each day. When the healing is complete, it is important to remove the crystals and wash them thoroughly, because they will have absorbed the negativity discharged from the chakra.

Crystals can be kept near your bed or at your desk, or worn around your neck on a chain. They may need to be cleansed from time to time by being placed under cold, running water. If you have worn a crystal for a period of time during stress or change, it is advised to give it time to discharge the negative energy it has absorbed. You can place your crystals in the freezer compartment of your refrigerator for a few days to let them "chill out."

Sounding the Chakras

Sound healing works on a similar principle to that of color healing. Each chakra resonates with a particular note of the musical scale. These notes can be sung, chanted, or chimed over the chakra to discharge energetic dross and open the chakra to a stronger energy flow. Sound is capable of healing our energy field as effectively as color; and, in combination with any one of the modalities mentioned earlier, it helps redress disharmony.

| Scale: middle C | Root Chakra: low C | Sacral Chakra: D | Solar Plexus Chakra: E | Heart Chakra: F | Throat Chakra: G | Brow Chakra: A | Crown Chakra: B |

USING THE NOTES

The Indian sitar is designed to bring healing to the chakras because it is tuned to all these notes. Ragas are composed for specific chakras, as well as played at specific times of the day when it would be most beneficial to listen to them. Harp music, too, can be used for healing the chakras, as one note is played repeatedly near the part of the body in need of tuning.

A good voice coach can help you make the specific sound of each note that would allow you to sound the chakras in yourself and for others. Being able to chant these notes is like giving yourself an internal chakra massage.

Food Therapy

The chakras resonate with specific foods that carry a vibration that heals and stabilizes them. When you wish to bring healing to a particular chakra, you may want to change the emphasis of your normal diet to include more of these food types.

The very process of grain production, from sowing and ripening to harvesting, reflects the bounty of our world. Simple foods such as grain remind us of our connection to the earth and help ground our spirit on the physical plane.

ROOT CHAKRA
Meats, chicken, and grains such as wheat, oats, and brown rice are beneficial. Red fruit such as apples, tomatoes, and red berries all carry the red energy of the Root Chakra. Also useful are national or religious dishes that convey community identity. Any favorite food from childhood can also stimulate the Root Chakra and is a reminder of a time the world was safe and carefree.

SACRAL CHAKRA
Fish, other seafood, algae, oranges, citrus, melons, sweet potatoes, squash, pumpkins, and carrots are all good for this center. Dishes that are sensuous to eat and stimulate the memory of good times are also beneficial.

SOLAR PLEXUS CHAKRA
Chicken, eggs, sunflower and olive oils, honey, molasses, pineapple, lemons, grapefruit, and brown rice are all good for this chakra and easy to digest. Food that is good against liver stagnation, such as green vegetables, and foods that aid digestion serve this chakra.

HEART CHAKRA

Heart of lamb, chicken, and beef are good
for the Heart Chakra, as are small amounts
of wine, sprouts, other greens, and low-fat
cottage cheese. Foods rich in omega fatty
acids such as salmon are good for the heart,
as well as foods that increase circulation.
The heart needs good nutrition to be strong.

THROAT CHAKRA

The Throat Chakra likes food that is easy to
swallow. It does not like mucous-producing
foods, such as chocolate, dairy products, or
excess candy. When the throat is sore, lemon
and honey are soothing.

BROW CHAKRA

In ancient times, salmon, tea, and almonds
were thought to be good for the brain.
Salmon was the fish of wisdom to the
ancient Celts. Aristotle said six almonds and
tea were good for the brain. Eating lightly
keeps the mind clear. Food that is fresh, free
of additives, and high in protein is excellent
for the Brow Chakra.

CROWN CHAKRA

Fasting is the "food" of the spirit. Occasional
fasts at changes of the seasons purify the
blood and open the spirit to changing earth
rhythms and cycles. Fasting helps us be
grateful for the abundance available to us
that we are able to choose from.

*Honey restores skin
tissue, purges the lungs,
and helps digestion.
It is used as a medium
for herbal essences and
homeopathic remedies.
It is absorbed easily and
can help heal all chakras.*

Meditation Using Angels, the Goddess, and the Christ Light

The five major archangels, the Goddess, and the Christ Light within us offer us guidance as we bring healing to the chakras. If you have a prayer for healing in one or another of the energy centers, offer your prayers to one of these divine aspects of self and allow them to deliver your prayers and intentions for healing to the source.

The Archangel Michael is the conqueror who fights for the good, the leader of the heavenly armies. He stands for courage, integrity, and justice. He is the patron saint of those who risk their lives for people.

ARCHANGEL MICHAEL
Michael corresponds to the Root Chakra. He brings us the challenge of making our life have purpose and meaning. He brings healing to the Root Chakra by helping us belong. If you have a prayer for belonging, healing your relationship with community, or finding your true path in life, address it to the Archangel Michael.

ARCHANGEL METATRON
Metatron corresponds to the Sacral Chakra. He teaches us to value the material world and to treat our resources carefully and with pride. He encourages us to love life in all its glory. When you have a need to pray for health issues, joy, abundance, and a wholesome sense of deservedness, address your prayers to the Archangel Metatron.

ARCHANGEL URIEL
Uriel corresponds to the Solar Plexus Chakra. He represents the power of our own true worth and encourages us to know ourselves. He can be called upon whenever

we are in doubt or experience fear or anxiety. If you have prayers to help you develop an abiding sense of well-being and to know your true identity, address them to the Archangel Uriel.

ARCHANGEL RAPHAEL
Raphael corresponds to the Heart Chakra. He brings us God's healing love, and shows us the herbs and medicines that we can use to bring balance and healing to our system. If you have prayers to mend a broken heart, to know love, and to give your best to those you love, address those prayers to Raphael.

ARCHANGEL GABRIEL
Gabriel corresponds to the Throat Chakra. He teaches us to honor truth and to oppose untruths. If you have a prayer to cultivate truth in your life and stop lying to yourself, or stop substance abuse, gossip, or spreading negativity, address your prayers to Gabriel.

THE SHEKHINAH
The Shekhinah, or feminine face of God, describes the Brow Chakra. She helps us to see the inner light in all things and to honor the best part of people. She teaches us to be discerning, intuitive, imaginative, and knowledgeable. If you have a prayer to cultivate wisdom and use it for healing, address it to the Shekhinah.

THE CHRIST LIGHT
The Christ Light corresponds to the Crown Chakra. This is the pure light within us that is permanent, ever radiant, and ever connected to the source of all life. When you have a prayer to know your true self in all its splendor, you can commune with that light to request healing, peace, and love.

Throughout history, people have believed in the importance of angels and they have featured heavily in art and architecture.

The Archangel Gabriel is known as the annunciator who bore the news of the coming birth of Christ to the Virgin Mary.

INDEX

A

activity: levels of 17
acupuncture 14, 50, 132
adrenals 19, 32
affirmations 7, 27, 39, 53, 67, 81, 95, 109, 121
agate: blue 97
Ajna 100
alexandrite 123
amber 69
amethyst 123
Anahata 72
ancestral roots 31
angels: meditation using 140–141
aquamarine 97
archetypes 18
aura 11–12
  layers 12–13
  strengthening 11
  visualizing 13

B

Bach flower remedies 133
balance 44, 115
bloodstone 41
brain: stimulating 100
Brow Chakra 15, 100–113
  accessing 108–109
  activities 17
  affirmations 109
  Ajna 100
  archetypes 18, 102
  associations 33–34
  attributes 101
  color 112
  crystals 111, 136
  Emotional Body and 105
  emotional energies 21
  foods 139
  functions 100–107
  glandular connection 19, 102
  meditation 110–111
  Mental Body and 106
  mental energies 22
  negative attitudes 109, 113
  Physical Body and 102
  physical energy 19
  positive attitudes 109
  qualities 101
  questionnaire on 112–113
  shape 110
  spiritual dimension 107
  symbol 7

C

chakras 9–27
  activity levels 17
  archetypes and 18
  balancing 135
  colors 12
  elements linked to 14
  emotional energies 21
  energy levels 14–15
  explaining 6
  feminine 15
  functions 16–23
  glandular connections 19
  intelligences 25
  masculine 15
  mental energies 22
  physical energies 19
  qualities 14
  sealing 135
  symbols 7
  visualizing 23
change: times of 34
choice 38, 66
  freedom of 63, 105
Christ Light 141
citrine 69
color healing 130–131
colors 12
confidence 62
consciousness:
  expanding 36
cornelian 55
Crown Chakra 114–125
  accessing 120–121
  activities 17
  affirmations 121
  archetypes 18, 116
  associations 117–118
  attributes 115
  color 124
  crystals 123, 136
  Emotional Body and 119
  emotional energies 21
  foods 139
  functions 114–118
  glandular connection 19, 116
  meditation 122–123
  Mental Body and 119
  mental energies 22
  negative attitudes 121, 125
  Physical Body and 116
  physical energy 19
  positive attitudes 121
  qualities 115
  questionnaire on 124–125
  Sahasrara 114
  shape 122
  spiritual dimension 119
  symbol 7
crystal healing 136
crystals 41, 55, 69, 83, 97, 111, 123

D

detoxification 129
diamond 83
discipline 51
divine guidance 118
Divine plane 12
dreams 128
duality 61
ductless glands 6

E

ego: healthy 64
electrical energies 15
elements: links to chakras 14
Emotional Body 12
  chakras and 21, 35, 49, 63, 77, 91, 105, 119
  emotional energies 21
  releasing 16
emotions: managing 21
endocrine glands 6
energies:
  electrical 15
  mental 22
  physical 19
energy:
  aura 11
  body as map of 19
  healing power of 20
  layers 11
  levels 14–15
  magnetic 15
  movement 11
  sensory 103
  subtle 10–15
energy conductors 16
energy fields 6
enlightenment 120